Emotional Intelligence

Journey To The Centre
Of Yourself

First published by O Books, 2009
O Books is an imprint of John Hunt Publishing Ltd., The Bothy, Deershot Lodge, Park Lane, Ropley,
Hants, SO24 0BE, UK
office1@o-books.net
www.o-books.net

Distribution in:	South Africa
	Alternative Books
UK and Europe	altbook@peterhyde.co.za
Orca Book Services	Tel: 021 555 4027 Fax: 021 447 1430
orders@orcabookservices.co.uk	
Tel: 01202 665432 Fax: 01202 666219	Text copyright Jane Wharam 2008
Int. code (44)	
	Design: Stuart Davies
USA and Canada	
NBN	ISBN: 978 1 84694 187 0
custserv@nbnbooks.com	
Tel: 1 800 462 6420 Fax: 1 800 338 4550	All rights reserved. Except for brief quotations
	in critical articles or reviews, no part of this
Australia and New Zealand	book may be reproduced in any manner without
Brumby Books	prior written permission from the publishers.
sales@brumbybooks.com.au	
Tel: 61 3 9761 5535 Fax: 61 3 9761 7095	The rights of Jane Wharam as author have been
	asserted in accordance with the Copyright,
Far East (offices in Singapore, Thailand,	Designs and Patents Act 1988.
Hong Kong, Taiwan)	
Pansing Distribution Pte Ltd	
kemal@pansing.com	A CIP catalogue record for this book is available
Tel: 65 6319 9939 Fax: 65 6462 5761	from the British Library.

Printed and bound by CPI Group (UK) Ltd., Croydon, CR0 4YY

O Books operates a distinctive and ethical publishing philosophy in
all areas of its business, from its global network of authors to
production and worldwide distribution.
This book is produced on FSC certified stock, within ISO14001
standards. The printer plants sufficient trees each year through
the Woodland Trust to absorb the level of emitted carbon in
its production.

Emotional Intelligence

Journey To The Centre
Of Yourself

Jane Wharam

BOOKS

Winchester, UK
Washington, USA

CONTENTS

Chapter 5 Acceptance And Understanding Of Emotions

Chapter 6 Self-mastery

Being In Control
The Authentic Self

Chapter 7 Emotions In Others

Chapter 8 Empathy

Chapter 9 Management & Motivation

INTRODUCTION

'Whatever you do will be insignificant, but it is most important that you do it.'
Gandhi (1869 –1948)

Congratulations! You have decided to change your life for the better and improve your Emotional Intelligence. It won't necessarily be easy and parts may be very difficult or even cause you temporary emotional pain but the journey will be worth it. By the end of this book you will be an expert on the most important thing in the world – You! No-one else can know you like you can; no-one else can delve as deep or be so honest. Tiny changes to the way you think and behave will make HUGE changes in your life.

So, what will you get out of reading this book? Well, you'll know a bit more about Emotional Intelligence generally, its history and the major players in the journey thus far; mainly though, you will find out about yourself, which emotions rage or flicker inside you and what to do with them if they erupt. You are about to go on a journey into the centre of yourself and you are the only person in the world who can do it. We can give you a compass of sorts and can ask you questions, but only you can supply the answers. Please don't think that this is just another from of navel-gazing. You are – or should be – the most important person in your life.

As Arnold Bennett said: *'If egotism means a terrific interest in one's self, egotism is absolutely essential to efficient living.'*

By taking baby steps – which get mentioned a lot, as it's the only way to travel – you will find that you:

- Know yourself better
- Identify what really turns you off and turns you on

1

- Improve your relationships
- Manage your own emotions and effectively deal with the emotions of others
- Communicate effectively and positively to influence others
- Increase flexibility, and effectively deal with conflict, change and growth
- Follow your instincts
- Curb impulsive behaviour and lessen the risk of Emotional Hijack

So, if that list rings your personal bell, start reading.......

Good luck!

Chapter 1

Emotional Intelligence

What Is Emotional Intelligence?

'There can be no knowledge without emotion.
We may be aware of a truth,
Yet, until we have felt its force,
It is not ours.
To the cognition of the brain must be added the experience of the soul.'
Arnold Bennett

As you will notice as you read on, we like Arnold Bennettt a lot. We also like Plato, Jung, Aristotle, Schiller, Daniel Goleman and anyone else who has contributed their words of wisdom to the great Emotional Intelligence debate, even if, when they wrote what they wrote, the term hadn't been coined.

We even like dry, dictionary definitions like this: *'the awareness of and ability to manage one's emotions in a healthy and productive manner.'*

The Psychology Dictionary definition of Emotional Intelligence

While the on-line encyclopaedia, Wikipedia, describes it as *'an ability, capacity, or skill to perceive, assess, and manage the emotions of one 's self, of others and of groups.'*

There are literally thousands of web pages on Emotional Intelligence and everyone wants to claim the right definition but how many definitions do we need?

In order to make this easier to read, let us deal with the

various terminologies now. Most writers on the subject inter-
change the terms **EQ** (Emotional Quotient) and **EI** (Emotional
Intelligence) and we are no exception. While EI is the technically
correct acronym to describe the concept, EQ has a catchier 'ring '
to it and because of its similarity to IQ, leads people to start
thinking about emotions, intelligence and the mind. When we use
the term EQ, then, we will be interchanging it with EI or
Emotional Intelligence, unless we state that we are talking about
the scale of measurement – but more of that later.

We believe that almost every person is born with a certain
innate potential for balanced Emotional Intelligence. We say
almost because there is still controversy surrounding certain types
of individual and the neurological wiring of their brain, such as
people on the autism spectrum disorder scale, although, as we go
to print, we are conducting pilot schemes with people at the
Aspergers end of the scale to see if they can learn emotional intelligence. If they can, then that's a whole new chapter. Just watch
this space.

This innate intelligence can be either developed or damaged
with life experiences, particularly by the emotional lessons
learned during childhood and adolescence. We say on the website
that people can have their EI rationalized out of them. This is very
common in the modern world, particularly in academic or scientific circles. Children behave as children should (hopefully) and
up to the age of three have little control over their emotions, yet
are usually told to 'behave' – ie. not to exhibit emotional
tendencies, like crying or anger. The constant dichotomy between
what a child feels and what a child is told is good behaviour, can
lead an intelligent child (especially) to suppress their emotions as
the years go on. (Maybe that's why the English middle classes
have the reputation of being such a buttoned-up repressed
bunch).

We also refer to EI being beaten out of a person. Unfortunately,
as with rationalisation, the children of abusive or neglectful

parents can also grow up believing that they should never show their true emotions, for different reasons – and it can start from birth.

Erik Erikson puts it in terms of a child learning 'basic trust or basic mistrust'. On the other hand, it has been observed in test studies in America for a child to start out with relatively low EI, but if they receive healthy emotional modeling and nurturing the result will be a moderately high EI. These results are proof that EI training can help a person learn and develop such traits as optimism or empathy.

The impact of these childhood lessons result in what is referred to as one's level of EQ as an adult. In other words, as we use the term, EQ represents a relative measure of a person's development of their innate emotional intelligence.

When we talk about EQ measurement, we are referring to scales, such as the Mayer, Salovey, Caruso Emotional Intelligence Test or MSCEIT, the BarOn Eqi Assessment or the 'Personality Test of General Emotional Intelligence' or GEIS. There are various of these scales in existence, just as there are with IQ. For those of you who like scores, why not find some on the internet and test yourself; it can be fun.

Generally speaking, the higher a person scores on any of the EI scales would mean that, against the average, they:

- Have better-developed levels of self-awareness – ie. they know themselves better
- Know what pushes their emotional buttons
- Know what motivates them
- Have a generally more cheerful or optimistic outlook
- Are more adaptable and happier to change
- Have relatively fewer emotional outbursts (Emotional Hijacks)
- Are not as repressed
- Have better self-discipline

- Are generally friendlier
- Have greater general self-esteem
- Live a more authentic life than most

We will explain the terms such as 'Emotional Hijack' and 'Authenticity' later in the book.

EQ versus IQ

This would probably be a good place to explain the difference between EQ and IQ. How often have you met people who are seemingly brilliant in terms of IQ and yet who can't maintain relationships or who seem to be misfits? On the other hand, how often do we meet people who are just wonderful at building rapport or maintaining friendships, who are nowhere near as bright or clever in the academic sense?

As Samuel Goldwyn famously said: *'Give me a smart idiot before a stupid genius any day'*.

One big difference is that relatively few people start out with high innate IQ, in maths, for example, and then have this ability damaged through misleading or false maths training. For example, in a classroom, a child is unlikely to be taught that that 2 + 2 equals 57.

On an emotional level however they can be taught inappropriate lessons, even when their parents have the best of intentions. Imagine, then, how damaged they can be at the hands of abusive parents or carers.

So, it could appear that EQ has little to do with IQ. However, it has been demonstrated, again in America, that children exhibiting higher EI at the age of four predicted a 210 point advantage in their SAT results at 18. We must stress though that you don't need to be Einstein to have a high level of Emotional Intelligence.

For the sake of good order, let us explain that the term *'emotional quotient'* or EQ seems to have originated in England in the 1980s in an article in Mensa's magazine by Keith Beasley.

Beasley's definition of the differences, particularly coming from someone with a very high IQ, is beautifully simple: *"EQ is probably best defined as one's 'ability to feel ', IQ being one's ability to think."*

Or, put another way, *"EQ is to the heart what IQ is to the brain."* Generally, psychological research demonstrates that IQ is a reliable measure of cognitive capacity (brightness in lay terms), and is stable over time. In the area of EQ however, definitions are inconsistent about what it measures; some say that EQ is dynamic, and can be learned or increased, whereas others (such as Mayer) say that EQ is stable, and cannot be increased. Our research and that of many others, such as Daniel Goleman, Reuven Bar-on and Beasley, would indicate that it can be learned – otherwise we wouldn't have written this book.

The History of Emotional Intelligence

In order to arrive at a commonly acceptable definition, let us examine the history of the concept. As far as we can make out, it all began about 2,000 years ago when Plato wrote: *'All learning has an emotional base.'*

Since then, scientists, psychologists, philosophers and spiritual leaders have worked to prove or disprove the importance of emotions in the development of the person.

In the 1950s, Abraham Maslow wrote about how people could enhance their emotional, physical, spiritual, and mental strengths and modelled this in his Hierarchy of Needs, which, on an earthly plane, culminated in 'self-actualisation'. His work was one of the sparks of the Human Potential Movement, which led to the development of many new sciences of human capacity.

Serious research was being done to define both emotions and intelligence. One of these researchers was Dr Peter Salovey, now Yale University's Psychology Department Chair. He says that over the last few decades, beliefs about emotions and intelligence have both changed; where intelligence was once viewed as perfection, people were recognizing that there was more to life. Where emotion was once perdition, people were recognizing that it might have value after all. It is amazing to us that emotions could ever have been discounted when applied to people, but that's science for you.

The story goes that Salovey and his friend, Dr John (Jack) Mayer were painting a room in Salovey's house in the late 1980s and began to discuss recent research in Intelligence and Emotions – but as separate entities, as the two were not thought to be in any way related. When asked later why they had thought to combine the two, Salovey joked, "Maybe it was the paint fumes!" Anyway, in 1990, their seminal paper first defined the concept of Emotional Intelligence as a scientifically testable 'intelligence'.

We say that they were the first, but in the early Sixties, Dutch science fiction author Carl Lans had published two novels in which he not only elaborates on the concept, he also actually uses the phrase Emotional Quotient. It is said that these books were never translated but since they later formed the basis of an immensely popular radio show, there is no way of knowing when the phrase found its way into English. Plus, given that the term IQ had been used since the early 1900s, it wouldn't have taken a creative genius to start referring to the measurement of emotional intelligence as EQ.

Emotional Intelligence In Its Modern Form

There are also numerous other assessments of emotional intelligence, each advocating different models and measures but the term was popularized by Daniel Goleman, who published his book Emotional Intelligence in 1995, which swept to the best seller lists for an amazing 80 weeks and sold over 5 million copies worldwide – an incredible feat for a book on an academic subject.

Goleman's own definition of EQ is *'the capacity for recognising our own feelings and those of others, for motivating ourselves and for managing emotions effectively in others and ourselves.'*

Goleman identified the five 'domains' or steps of Emotional Intelligence as:

- Knowing your emotions
- Managing your own emotions
- Motivating yourself
- Recognizing and understanding other people's emotions
- Managing relationships – ie. managing the emotions of others

Salovey and Mayer's definition is slightly more complicated: *'Emotional intelligence is the ability to perceive emotions; to access and generate emotions so as to assist thought; to understand emotions and emotional knowledge; and to reflectively regulate emotions so as to promote emotional and intellectual growth.'*

In other words, there are four parts or 'domains' in their definition:

- Perceive or sense emotions
- Use emotions to assist thought
- Understand emotions
- Manage emotions.

It's interesting to note that, back in the 1960s, Maslow had laid out his Hierarchy of Needs in a very similar, stepped fashion, saying much the same thing. The top of the pyramid, Self-Actualisation, has the following steps:

1. Awareness
2. Honesty
3. Freedom
4. Trust

Maslow's Hierachy of Needs

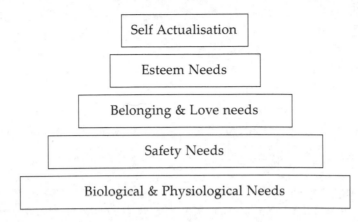

So, what does it matter who has said what and when? We shall see. While some researchers have focused on defining the skills of emotional intelligence, others have looked at the effects, sensibly in our opinion, as, after all, what use is theory without practice? Reuven Bar-On has been interested in emotional skills since the mid-1980s. He developed a test that measures people's self-report of these competencies (we call them skills) called the EQ-i. We will look at self-assessment later in the book.

We go into some depth in this history section, as the very debate is an example of EI at work – or not – in our opinion. Salovey and Mayer are said to feel dismayed at how Goleman 'distorted' their original theory on Emotional Intelligence, going so far as to wail 'It's not true!' Our answer is, so what? There can be no true or correct definition. We're talking about theories after all. It's not the Intelligentsia versus the emotionally incontinent! All we're saying is that a balance would be nice. But then what do we know? We're just lay people trying to apply common sense! But, maybe we're not so wide of the mark. As Salovey and Mayer's colleague David Caruso writes, *'It is very important to understand that emotional intelligence is not the opposite of intelligence, it is not the triumph of heart over head – it is the unique intersection of both.'*

Indeed, Doctors Salovey and Mayer seem to have come round to our way of thinking a little more of late, so let us give the last word to Dr Salovey. In a recent paper he wrote: 'I think in the coming decade we will see well-conducted research demonstrating that emotional skills and competencies predict positive outcomes at home with one 's family, in school, and at work. The real challenge is to show that emotional intelligence matters over-and-above psychological constructs that have been measured for decades like personality and IQ. I believe that emotional intelligence holds this promise.'

Our Definition of Emotional Intelligence

We may as well throw our own definition into the pot. As we have stated, in our opinion, the concept or theory of Emotional Intelligence really boils down to common sense and keeping a sense of balance; however, the *skills* required to use EI successfully may need to be learned or developed. By developing our Emotional Intelligence we can become more productive and successful at what we do and how we interact with others, and even help others to be more productive and successful too, which mirrors Maslow's theory of self-actualisation.

At present, all other models of emotional intelligence combine the measurement of the innate emotional variables such as sensitivity, memory, processing and learning with the environmental effects on those same variables. The common words across all the definitions seem to be 'awareness', 'manage', 'emotions', 'self' and 'others'; therefore our nutshell definition of Emotional Intelligence is:

'The potential to be aware of and use one 's own emotions in communication with oneself and others and to manage and motivate oneself and others through understanding emotions.'

Why Is Emotional Intelligence Important?

'No man is an island... I am involved in mankind'
John Donne

It is true that none of us lives in isolation and to progress in every way in the world, which is made up of mankind, we must fit in with each other. Think about what makes us get on with other people. We constantly make judgments about people; about whether we like them or not. These judgments are mainly really emotional reflexes, (or gut feelings) of which we are rarely conscious but are nonetheless so powerful that they motivate many of our choices in life. When they are triggered we can either react to people and situations in a negative way or we can respond with awareness, sensitivity, and balance.

Being aware of these emotional reflexes and using them in a positive and healthy way can make the difference between an emotionally intelligent person and one who isn't. However, when making judgments, just remember what Arnold Bennett said: *'It is well, when judging a friend, to remember that he is judging you with the same godlike and superior impartiality.'*

Emotional intelligence, though, is far more than being 'nice' to people, which is what Salovey and Mayer accused Goleman of saying. It is based on both scientific discoveries of how the brain works and workplace studies in a wide variety of industries and job categories. According to Goleman, of all the skills needed for success in life and business, over 60% are emotional. We're not sure where he gets this information from but it does seem evident that cognitive intelligence alone is no indicator of success. Think about a job interview. If a company wants to hire a new member of staff they first of all draw up a list of qualities that the person should possess. Firstly, there has to be a level of intelligence, often measured by qualifications, then there is a level of experience in the field of work, and finally interpersonal skills. So, from a pool of similarly qualified people with similar levels of experience, they will probably choose the one who interviews best – it's as simple as that. To be pejorative, they won't hire a 'boffin' or an obvious emotional mess.

Emotional Intelligence is also all about making choices. According to Byron Stock, you can use the information about what you're feeling to help you make effective decisions about what to say or do (or not say or do) next.

He says: *'Emotional Intelligence is not about being soft! It is ...having the skill to use your emotions to help you make choices in-the-moment and have more effective control over yourself and your impact on others.'*

In our opinion, emotional intelligence is also about being happy in one's own skin, although Goleman doesn't talk much about the pursuit of happiness in his book, which we find rather strange. It is also interesting to note that both Goleman and Mayer & Salovey omit the word 'healthy'. Surely healthy and positive are pre-requisites of intelligence? How many self help books have we all read that say that in order to love someone else we first have to learn to love ourselves? People high in emotional intelligence are strong at identifying their own emotions and others' emotions, expressing emotions, managing emotions and integrating emotions with their thoughts and behaviour. We're back to the balance between rational and analytical thought and reacting to everything in an over-emotional way.

Emotional Intelligence training is important because it *works* and can make a huge difference to stress and well-being. There have been many well-documented studies of its effectiveness, mainly in business, in America but one nearer to home was conducted a few years ago in a large supermarket chain by Dr Mark Slaski of the University of Hertfordshire.

To test the theory, a group of 60 managers were trained for one day per week for four weeks. Assessments were taken prior to the training that included two measures of EQ, general health, stress, distress, quality of working life and morale. In addition, each participant's line-manager was asked to evaluate the trainee using the organisation 's own management performance measure. The programme was created to help managers understand their own emotional responses and how they relate to their own thoughts and behaviour. Also, how to identify the characteristics of their own self-aspects using emotions, and to manage others on this 'values' based level. Six months after the completion of the training, measurements were taken once again. Results showed that managers on the training course, over and above those who did not take part, significantly increased their:

- EQ (score)
- General health
- Morale
- Quality of working life
- Performance
- Significantly reduced stress and distress.

Again in the UK, in 2006 the then DfES conducted pilot schemes in schools around the country in the Social and Emotional Aspects of Learning or SEAL, which are loosely based on Emotional Intelligence training. The results were so positive that SEAL is to be incorporated into the national curriculum from September 2007. After the pilots it was reported that:

- In Plymouth, three schools saw serious behaviour incidents go down, and a drop in fixed-term and lunchtime exclusions.
- In Southend, seven out of the nine pilot schools saw improvements in KS2 maths and English results.
- In Cornwall, nine out of the ten pilot schools rep

improvements in children's ability to co-operate and communicate.

It would appear, then, that Emotional Intelligence training has been proven to have a positive impact on behaviour, attitudes and learning ability, which can only be good for the individual and society.

Like Maslow's self-actualisation, we believe it is a natural progression for us. It must be for you too, or you wouldn't have read this far. Perhaps we are striving for a work/life balance, maybe, dare we say it, we are looking for a balance between the head, the heart and the soul.

Chapter 2

Emotions

What Are Emotions?

'There can be no transforming of darkness into light and of apathy into movement without emotion.'
Jung

It is interesting that Jung uses the word 'movement' when he talks of transformation, as Daniel Goleman points out that the word 'emotion' comes from the Latin 'e' or out of' and 'motere' meaning motion. We have already discussed the concept that emotions impel a person to 'do' something physical, whether it be to hit someone across the face with a wet fish or simply to start sweating and it would appear that emotions are the most basic and powerful tool we possess to make us do things. While highly emotional states are usually accompanied by action, it could just as well be a withdrawal that occurs, a retreat into an inner, safer world – curling up into a ball and closing one's eyes. Either way, it's physical.

At any one point, the human being is teeming with emotions. Let's go back to definitions again. To Wikipedia, emotion is: *'the language of a person's mental state of being, normally based in or tied to the person's internal (physical) and external (social) sensory feeling.'*

You have heard the expression 'emotional vocabulary'; this refers to being able to label the feelings – another word for emotions – a person is experiencing. It is also referred to as *emotional literacy*. These emotions/feelings could be misery, euphoria, sadness or any one of the hundreds of feelings a person experiences at any time. Most feelings are reactive – ie. another person says or does something that invokes a feeling in the first person. The reason why most people's emotions are reactive is that few people reflect quietly on themselves – possibly because they are too afraid of what they might experience within themselves if they do. So, they distract themselves with alcohol, drugs, sex, TV or a host of other diversions – anything is better than examining what they are actually *feeling*. Then, when confronted with an event they can't escape, either verbal or physical, they experience a (usually strong) emotion and react to it without thinking about what it is they are experiencing, whether it is an appropriate emotion for the circumstances or whether their reaction to it is in proportion with the event itself. Does the phrase, she 'lashed out' sound familiar?

Aristotle put it in a nutshell, using the emotion of anger when he said: '*Anybody can become angry, that is easy; but to be angry with the right person, and to the right degree, and at the right time, and for the right purpose, and in the right way, that is not within everybody's power, that is not easy.*'

And it's that proportionality or balance between heart and head that we are aiming for in this book.

Remember what Beasley said about EQ being to the heart what IQ is to the brain? In his chapter on emotions in the 1995 book, Goleman uses the slightly more literary example of Antoine de St Exupéry, who, in his book The Little Prince said: '*It is with the heart that one sees rightly; what is essential is invisible to the eye.*'

Emotions or passions, as Jung calls them, are much older in terms of evolution than intelligent or rational thought, which tends to focus on what we can prove, see, hear, touch or taste. In fact, according to neuro-scientists, who can now monitor the brain while a person is conscious, it can be proven that emotions in evolutionary terms are very old, and that emotional processing is pre-linguistic and therefore more universal and symbolic in nature.

This may explain the power of emotions over logic. Think about Captain Kirk and Mr Spock. Spock was incapable of feeling emotion, which is what made him so different and feared by the humans. His mind was purely logical, while the thinking part of Kirk's mind could (and often was) hijacked by his emotional responses to the set of circumstances at the time.

We mentioned Plato at the beginning and that scientists have tried to prove or disprove the power of emotions ever since. Very often, in this rational world, it has not been acceptable to admit to having emotions and, as we have mentioned before, they have been bred out of many people, causing untold psychological problems. Fortunately, in the last thirty years or so, there has been a change in attitude and seemingly 'rational people have started to balance logic with emotion. But is it really possible to think clearly (rationally) when in an emotional state, as Aristotle advocates? We would say yes, but usually only with practice and we talk about situations where emotion overcomes reason in the section on Emotional Hijack.

The Core Emotions

It doesn't matter how intelligent a person is; faced with imminent and powerful life-threatening danger, they will still soil themselves in order to make their body lighter for running away. That is a hard-wired response from the origins of man. However, science suggests that there are only a handful of core emotions. This has been described by many researchers and relates to the fact that there are only five or six universally-recognised emotional facial expressions – which, presumably, in evolutionary terms, come from pre-historic times. These are:

- Fear
- Anger
- Disgust
- Sadness
- Surprise
- Joy

This is not to say that emotions such as embarrassment, shame or envy are not real emotions, but these tend to be more complicated and generally involve thinking about a set of circumstances, rather then being immediate emotional responses, and are therefore considered as secondary. Maybe we could say that the first six are instinctive and don't involve thought while the other emotions contain greater or lesser degrees of analysis.

So, if there are only a handful of core emotions, then what is their function? Fear and anger are strongly related to the flight, fight or freeze response, and prepare the body for action in the face of threat or danger. In other words, feeling these emotions can literally save your life.

Disgust is a physical emotion to do with getting rid of poisoned or tainted food or water – again potentially life-threatening. You only have to ask someone to smell rotting food to elicit the disgust response; it involves the screwing up of the face and tight closing of mouth and nostrils – that's not entering my body!

Sadness is related to loss, and one of humanity's biggest instincts is aversion to loss. In prehistoric man any physical loss, say through injury, could have proved fatal to the individual, and in this sense the emotion of sadness is associated with withdrawal, shutting down systems and seeking support during a period of repair and recuperation.

Ultimately, humans behave in a way to avoid these negative, core emotions and thus preserve some measure of safety and security. Emotions may then be considered as guidance or warning systems. It is interesting to note that joy is usually only present in the absence of the other emotions. If we refer again to Maslow's hierarchy of needs, it is borne out by this, inasmuch as joy can only be experienced when the basic needs for security are met. This may explain why people at the very bottom of the pile find it hard to be joyful – although there are startling exceptions to this rule, which we will go into later.

According to researchers at the University of Hertfordshire, 21st Century Man is really a 'space-age man with a stone-age constitution'. But what are the real threats in modern life? Yes, physical threat still exists, but we are no longer faced by the same dangers experienced by our ancestors. Our emotions today are aroused by threats to a different part of us.

For the average person in the western world, rather than to our physical bodies, threat and challenge to our psychological and social selves are far more likely to lead us to experience fear, anger, disgust and sadness. We have largely replaced physical threat with a personal framework such as our own values, attitudes, beliefs, hopes, dreams, fears, expectations, goals and social position. Although these are almost entirely perceptions rather than reality, sure enough, if any of these aspects of ourselves are threatened we usually react with a negative emotional response of some sort – mental or physical flight, fight or freeze.

Emotions Generally

As we have said before, we are looking for a balance between emotionality and rational thought. George Orwell was spot on when he satirized pendulum swingers – ie. leaders who fastened onto a theory, which immediately took precedence over the previous one – 'Two legs bad, four legs good', or the other way round depending on which way the wind is blowing. Our modern, educated, rational society has seemingly dismissed emotions, giving credibility only to rational thought. Think of the stiff upper lip mentality, which causes so many breakdowns in later life. Thankfully, during the last several years or so, with the plethora of self-help manuals and spiritual guides in circulation we have seen a sea change, and more and more people are reassessing their feelings about feelings and are seeing them as a potential source of value. The new thought processes are:

- "If I don't deal with feelings now, they will cause me problems later in life."
- Feelings are a valuable guide in decision-making.
- There is more to life than the mind. Where does spirituality fit in?

We may even go a step further and say that our very consciousness is created by emotion; it's your feelings that create the awareness of your life – ie. you write your own script. That is something of a controversial viewpoint, which is being hotly debated currently. There are thousands of books on the subject, some of which are mentioned in the Recommended Reading section. All we would say here is that, without emotion, we would actually lose all perspective of what's important in life and almost all of the richness of life's experience. Imagine a life without joy, love, compassion or even sadness. Would it really be worth living?

In many cases, life's lessons from early childhood taught us that feelings were in the way of clear thinking, and often we learned to put them aside. It became obvious that we shouldn't vent our feelings and we should certainly never talk about them. If that was the case with you – and it certainly was with us – then listening to your emotions as adults becomes somewhat more challenging. So we need to understand the flow of feeling and thought.

Thinking of it in Eastern terms, it is like Yin and Yang. The Yin, or female force, represents 'being' and the Yang, or male force, represents 'doing'. Both are equally valid as separate entities but what we are aiming for is the union of those two forces in harmony and balance.

As you read on and explore the ways you're experiencing and using emotion, you may find yourself resisting approaching or actually feeling some feelings. You may even have learned somewhere that they are wrong or bad or dangerous. This may be because you have had a brush with emotions like lust or despair for example, and having experienced a tiny bit of the power in them, thought 'I'm not going there again!'

You're not being a coward; it's very hard to fully experience feelings that we suspect to be unsafe. As we explained earlier, our emotional brain is all about safety and avoiding loss, so it will resist when you engage in 'unsafe' feelings such as sorrow, grief or rejection. If you've decided that grief is dangerous, when you try to feel desolate you may find yourself doing almost anything but. People are incredibly good at resisting what they fear and will do almost anything to avoid it. However, the very reason you're reading this book, we suspect, is that you feel ready to confront your demons, so, here goes…

Quick Exercise – EI Journal

There are lots of these quick exercises dotted through the book and this is one of the most fundamental, as you will be doing it throughout your reading and, hopefully, for the rest of your lives. It may seem simple but keeping a journal was a major contributor to changing the life of the author – thanks, Sharon.

Buy a hardcover, blank page journal or get someone to give you one as a present. Make it completely personal to you and keep it somewhere where you know no-one else will be able to read it by mistake – we can't legislate for the snoopers in your life!

Every time you experience a strong emotional response – crying at a film or music, losing your temper, not losing your temper but wanting to, having a strong impulse to do or say something – write down the basic facts in the journal and date the entry. Don't re-live the incident, just make it as accurate a representation as you can. Also, try and divorce the emotion from the trigger. For example, you may have watched a film and cried at it but what were you crying about? Was it that Lassie came home or the death of your own pet as child, which was swept under the carpet and never dealt with? Following your instincts, which will become stronger as time goes on, write down how you feel and any snippets of dreams you remember. You will be amazed in time, when you re-read, how your attitudes have changed from today on.

Emotions Within Oneself – Learning the Skills

You will have seen from the preceding headings that the subject of Emotional Intelligence can be as complicated and scientific as you want to make it. Our approach, however, is that we just want to get on with ourselves and each other better, so we try and leave models of the scientific kind to the theorists or those who want to treat the human brain as if it was a computer. It's not. For one thing, it's much more versatile. The average person may not be able to define Pi to be precise to 40 digits but s/he can usually tell the difference between a genuine and heartfelt 'thanks' and a sarcastic one. However, scientific models can be useful, as they give us headings for what we need to *learn*. As we saw under Definitions, Goleman's model measures the EQ *skills* (our italics) as:

(please note that in American texts these are usually called *competencies*)

- Self-Awareness
- Self-Management
- Social Awareness
- Relationship Management

Whereas Salovey & Mayer say that they are:

- Perception, Appraisal and Expression of Emotion
- Emotional Facilitation of Thinking
- Understanding and Analysing Emotions; Employing Emotional Knowledge
- Reflective Regulation of Emotions to Promote Emotional and Intellectual Growth

We gravitate nearer to Goleman, but only because he has made it slightly less complicated. Thus, the skills we believe a person needs to learn are:

- Feeling Emotions / Self-awareness
- Identification and labeling of emotions / Emotional literacy
- Acceptance and understanding of emotions, including self-esteem
- Self-mastery (management) and the authentic self
- Management and motivation of others through effective communication

Chapter Three

Self-Awareness

How Well Do You Know Yourself?

'A person who has not passed through the inferno of their passions has never overcome them.'
Jung

As we mentioned in the last section, examining one's emotions is very hard to do and many – we hesitate to say most – people don't ever do it. 'I'm fine' or 'Let's just get on with it' are common responses. The problem is that we are *afraid* of confronting our emotions – as Jung says, it's an inferno in there! Isn't it strange that an emotion can be so powerful as to stop a person experiencing another emotion? Fear is one of the strongest emotions we possess. How many times have we not said or done something because we were afraid of the outcome if we did? Facing our fears, however, can be the most wonderful experience – knowing that we are in control of our emotion and not fear in control of us.

Quick exercise – 'So, what are my options if…?'

There is an excellent exercise for confronting fear (and other dangerous emotions) and we call it the 'So, what are my options if…?'

Let's say you're in debt and an envelope arrives, which looks horribly like a final demand. You're so afraid that you can 't even bring yourself to open the envelope – been there, done that. Your hands start to sweat and you feel anxiety in your guts; opening the envelope becomes a bigger hurdle and you're sure you know what's written inside it – you still can't bring yourself to open it.

Sit down with a sheet of paper and write out various scenarios associated with the contents of the letter.

'So, what are my options if.... it says they 're going to send the bailiffs in?'

'So, what are my options if ....it says they're going to add interest at silly %?'

'So, what are my options if.... they are going to destroy my credit rating?'

Now ask yourself, 'If I open this letter and it contains any of the above, or something similar, am I going to die or be badly damaged? Will anyone I love die or be badly damaged?'

The answer is no, isn't it? And, if the answer is no, which it almost always will be, in any situation, then you can deal with that situation, having already confronted the fear and looked at your options. This isn't the book to give specific answers to problems; all we would say in financial situations (which are all too common in this society) is, don't bury your head in the sand and do keep communication going. Most debtors will accept £5 a week rather than worry that their debt will never be paid.

There are hundreds of examples we could use for the 'So, what are my options if...' exercise. No doubt you have at least one on your mind now – unfortunately, that's how many of us in dire circumstances live our lives. We do promise, however, that it you practice this exercise you will start to feel more in control of yourself.

Another good way of helping you cope is to write your problems down on a time line, so that you aren't besieged by everything all at once. Take Scarlett O'Hara's advice, when she said:

'I won't think about that now. I'll think about that tomorrow.'

Quick Exercise – Clearing The Brain

Draw a line starting with now or today on the left and then list the days, weeks or months going to the right. It might look something like this:

Monday	Tuesday	Wednesday	Thursday	Friday	Saturday	Sunday
Send Cheque			Cheque clears			Get paid

Let's say that a credit card company wants you money by the 15th. Work backwards to the day you have to write and send your cheque so that it clears by that date. It's effectively a list of what you need to do, in what order at that particular time. This is a very basic example but it helps to get whatever your problem is clear in your head. Once something is committed to paper it's out of your brain and can be ticked off on your list of things to do; you have been pro-active instead of reactive, thus freeing your mind to be either still or creative, not going round in circles. Worrying about something just causes illness and doesn't achieve anything. If you prioritise your problems, allocate them the time to deal with them and then put them in the 'done' section, you're taking control back for yourself.

Your Inner Child

In order to develop your EI and Awareness you will need to have an understanding of the emotional processes that got you to where you are today and for the purposes of this book we are starting in childhood. Some would say that they start in the womb, but that's another debate entirely.

Born rich, poor, bright, less bright, physically able or not, we all start out in life as babies. We can only survive if fed and looked after by our parents or carers. If we are cared for physically but

27

not given any emotional nurturing, some emotional part of us withers and can die.

If you imagine a child's personality as being made up of tiny seedlings, it might make it easier. Let's say that, of the hundreds of seedlings making up the whole, some are fed and watered more than others. What we would be looking for in an emotionally intelligent person in later life is a row of seedlings of the same height and sturdiness; however, what we often find is an uneven, unbalanced-looking row, with some seedlings almost dead.

What happens is that every time any of these emotional needs is unmet, we lock that facet of our intelligence away and often throw away the key. Unfortunately, some of these emotional events occurred before we were three years old and so we have little or no recollection of them – or have buried them, again for our own self-protection. Most people's memories only go back to when they were three or three years of age, so for now, we will concentrate on how you developed your emotions from then.

In Recovery of your Inner Child Lucia Capacchione writes, " … *the inner child never grows up and never goes away. It remains buried alive, waiting to be set free. We can't build a truly workable, happy adult world on the shaky foundations of a frightened and isolated child who never got its basic needs met."*

We can only agree. If you've read this far, the chances are you can remember times when you felt lost, insecure or rejected as a child. Maybe some of those feelings have stayed with you into adult life? Don't worry, we can help you to address them.

As adults, sometimes events occur which trigger the feelings we locked away – they could be of guilt, rejection, blame, sadness or anxiety. Often we don't even know that these feelings are caused by the old scars from childhood; we think that it's just how we are. We then often repeat the same old patterns, as these dreadful feelings, however much misery they cause us, at least represent security. Thus the daughters of wife beaters often marry wife beaters or the sons of women haters often abuse their partners. In order to break these chains which bind us, we have to dig down and re-discover the injured child within and help it to come to terms with the adult world.

If you accept that you need to re-parent the child within, you first have to find a safe way of doing so. Everyone needs to feel safe in order to open up and if they do not feel safe they can be inclined to bury their feelings even deeper. Remember that we are programmed to resist pain, as it could mean loss, which could mean death. Consequently, getting that key out and unlocking that door, behind which are so many painful lessons and emotions can be too daunting for some people. If you really feel that you can't face doing so, it's probably an indicator that you aren't ready just yet. But, the fact that you are reading this book hopefully means that you can do this work and will find enormous benefit from it.

If you don't feel ready, willing, or safe enough to really get into the exercises later in the book, just reading this section thoroughly can be very useful and increase your self-under-standing. If your childhood was emotionally difficult or unhappy, going back and acknowledging what was too painful to feel before is difficult and courageous. It is entering into the inferno. Well done if you do and no shame if you can't. Some wounds are so deep that they may take a lifetime to be acknowledged, let alone heal.

Why Bother Going Back To Childhood?

Because someone has to break the chain. Let's say that someone has been rejected as a child by a significant figure in their lives. Those people will often use the withdrawal of love and affection as a weapon or defence mechanism in later life. They can then reject their own children or children close to them and the cycle starts all over again. Until someone in the chain learns that this is not a healthy emotional response, the cycle will go on and on and many people's lives will be ruined as a result.

If we do not do the work of healing our wounded inner child, the pain that remain below the surface can contaminate our lives and the lives of others. How many of us just keep playing the same old record and conforming to the same old pattern within ourselves and in relationships?

Ironically, however, it is often what we are not aware of that controls us. Through self-awareness we can exercise self-control and make better choices. Despite different theoretical approaches, all serious researchers in this field maintain that being aware of yourself in terms of 'who you are' and 'where you are going' is key to emotional intelligence.

People with high EQ tend to have a strong understanding of their values and beliefs, have clear goals and visions, have self-confidence and accept their strengths and weaknesses; they use their emotional experiences to better manage relationships and to guide their own behaviour. As a consequence they are better able to regulate and express their own emotions, and are less likely to be overwhelmed by stress. Moreover, they are capable of reading the deeper emotional meanings of others with whom they interact, and we will come back to that later. When we are more self-aware we can be more empathic and sensitive to the needs of others. With empathy and self-management we can positively influence others.

So, being self-aware is having the skills to focus your attention on your emotional state. Being aware, *in-the-moment*, of what you're feeling. Are you happy, excited, worried, angry? Given that information about your emotional state, what should (or shouldn't) you do or say next? Use that information to help you make effective decisions to achieve better outcomes for yourself and others. Self-awareness also helps us to identify emotion in our physical states, feelings, and thoughts. For example, if we suddenly find that we are tapping our fingers on the table, we may be feeling impatient. If our heart starts beating faster, coupled with a dry mouth, we are probably feeling fear. If we are constantly tired and have a knotted feeling in our stomachs, we are likely to be stressed or anxious. We can use these physical feelings as a barometer of our emotions, once we are aware of them.

So, you've taken a snapshot of your emotions and you've realised certain things about yourself and the way you behave. If you were once sure of the direction your life was going to take and were excited and optimistic about that but have now lost that direction and that buzz, can you get excited again? Can you get your life back on track?

To answer that question, it helps to understand the internal processes associated with getting excited, or feeling optimistic and joyful. This sounds simpler than it is because, as we pointed out earlier, few people ever venture 'inside'.

A person with high emotional self-awareness understands the internal process associated with emotional experiences and, therefore, has greater control over them. He or she can change the mood they're in by a series of simple exercises. We are all at the mercy of mood swings, except that in some people, bad moods can last for hours, days or weeks, while others can seemingly 'snap out' of them very quickly. In an effort to learn how to rise up the scale from depression to joy – impossible in a single leap but possible in small steps – try the following exercise:

Quick Exercise – the Mood Lifter

It has been shown in polls that when people are down it helps them to either talk to a friend, listen to music or take exercise. Let's assume that your friends aren't around and your CD player is broken – what do you do?

First of all, try and work out why you 're feeling low. It might be something really specific, such as bad news or something more nebulous, like the feeling after waking from a vivid dream, which you can't shake off. Either way, analyse exactly what you're feeling and why you think you're feeling it – ie. 'I feel disappointed because I didn't get that job' or 'I have a nasty feeling in the pit of my stomach, like before an exam. It's anxiety.'

Now imagine what you would say to a friend if they came to you and said exactly what you've just said to yourself. You wouldn't leave them in their disappointment or anxiety, would you? You would offer help and advice.

Next time you have a strong, unpleasant emotional feeling, like disappointment, for a specific reason, take yourself out of the situation and look at it dispassionately. Did your friend not get the job because they weren't really qualified for it? If so, suggest that they take adult education classes or volunteer in a similar business.

Did they not get it because their CV let them down? Tell them that there are loads of free CV writing tips out there to help with that. Maybe they didn't get the job because, of the sheer numbers of people who applied, only one person could be successful; it's nothing personal if they've done everything else right. Or, if the reason for the feeling is harder to pinpoint, remind them that it was only a dream, or a feeling and get them to remember and experience, as vividly as possible, a really happy time in their lives.

Once they are really immersed in the new thoughts, the old ones will evaporate and the beauty of it is that you know everything about them, so they can't lie to you! The point is that, having identified the unpleasant emotion, *you are doing something to alter it.*

As Samuel Goldwyn once said so eloquently: *'The harder I work, the luckier I get.'*

If you are more of a doer than an analyser, concentrate on some exercise, even if it's only lifting your arms or legs for a count of 10 at a time or exercising your pelvic floor. While you are exercising, try some 'I am' visualisations. These are a great way to boost one's self-confidence and thereby improve one's mood. With each physical repetition or muscle control movement, say 'I am alive and I am improving in every way. 'Best of all, say this out loud – not if you're in the library, obviously! Try and fit the 'I am' statement to the feeling you wish to change. For example, if you are feeling disappointed about the job, say "I am more experienced at looking for work every day."

Concentrate on what you want rather than on what you lack. Visualise your first day in your new job. There are more examples of visualisations in the visualisation section, funnily enough, on page 75.

SWOON

'People will do anything, no matter how absurd, to avoid facing their own soul.'
Jung

Self-awareness helps people to identify gaps in their interpersonal skills, which promote skill development. But self-awareness also helps people to find and discover situations in which they will be most effective, assists with their intuitive decision-making, and aids stress management and motivation of themselves and others.

Just for a moment, think about who you are. The usual tendency is to recite a list of positive, or negative (depending on your frame of mind) attributes to create a 'you' template. But how well do you actually know yourself? For example, you may think of yourself as a timid person, who suddenly finds herself furiously berating someone for being cruel to an animal or you may think of yourself as the strong, silent type, who unexpectedly weeps buckets at a sad film. Do you see yourself as others see you? Who are you?

If asked to describe a friend, people will often say that the other person is a salesman or policeman. But that 's not actually true, is it? That's not what the person is but more accurately what they do, and this is an important distinction. If we fail to make it, we get lost in the identity of our labels – lawyer, accountant, film star, politician, husband, housewife, editor, expert and even student and child. All of these are just describing words and probably only describe aspects of our personality anyway.

Think of the Krays. It has always been said, often in the same breath, that they were vicious gangsters, who disfigured people for showing disrespect, but unfailingly loved and protected their old mum. These facets may represent a portion of how we express ourselves in our world, but ultimately not who we truly are. No wonder we can feel dissatisfied with our lives; our labels of identity create our own imprisonment.

Quick exercise – labelling

Imagine you are sitting on a windswept beach somewhere you love. Make it your favourite time of the year. The tide is coming in and the sound of the surf on the shore fills the air. What word would you use to describe the ocean? Powerful? Majestic? Awesome? Frightening? Bleak? Wild? Uninviting? Cold? Cruel? Then again you may see the sunlight glint off the breakers, and you may love surfing, so the descriptive words may become Exciting, Breathtaking, Challenging, Inviting, Creative or even Empowering. And we can choose many other descriptions, such as Deep, Passionate, Energetic, Romantic... You choose your descriptions. Whatever you call it, it's the same sea...

Now, focus within and see *yourself* as the ocean. Imagine your mind like a powerful beam of light, arcing round a lighthouse. As your light sweeps the ocean, focus on one facet of your personality within it, choose a word to describe that bit of you. Then choose another and another. You may begin with descriptions of your body, then your mind, your emotions, your intellect, your education, or your history. Each part is only part of the whole and yet the whole is you – good, bad and neutral, brilliant, dull and colourless. None of us is made up wholly of good or bad; we're just all an amalgam of various parts, all shades of so many different colours.

As the ocean encompasses all possibilities and potential, so do we; it simply depends on where we choose to focus our attention.

And, as a last thought, we keep using facets of your personality. What else has facets? Yes, precious gems, and that's how you started out in this journey of life and could be again.

You may have wondered why this section is entitled SWOON. SWOON will help you become more self-aware. Just as we did with the lighthouse, we are now going to imagine ourselves as a product – we'll call it a You – and, remember, it should be a brilliant, shining gemstone. And for this exercise, we have to sell our You to the hardest market to crack – ourselves. Like any good marketers, we firstly need to do an analysis on the product, only instead of SWOT or PEST, we are going to SWOON – we are talking about emotions after all!

Get some A4 paper and, displaying it in landscape format, draw up the following grid:

Strengths				
Kind				
Loyal				
Funny				
Intelligent				

Strengths

What are the good points of the You? Come on, you made it, after all! You know everything there is to know about it. It may be well-hidden under a tough exterior but there may be a good dollop of Romantic hidden in there or a strong streak of Compassionate. Put the You under a microscope and write down every single strength it has, however small or under-developed.

When you have exhausted the Strengths column – and we hope you've had to use more paper, because this You is an excellent product, fill in the next column, so that your grid looks like this:

Strengths	Weaknesses			
Kind	Obstinate			
Loyal	Dithery			
Funny	Pedantic			
Intelligent	Habits			

Weaknesses

Now do the same exercise with the weaknesses of the you as you did with the Strengths. Initially, you may find this column easier to fill in but, ironically, what you will find if you enter into the exercise as thoughtfully as you can, is that focussing on the weaknesses will highlight strengths you may have missed, so add them in to the appropriate column. Another way of adding to the Strengths column is to look at the flipside of each weakness. Let's say, for example that you have written 'Dithery' in the weaknesses column. Is that all bad? If the You is dithery, could it also mean that it won't be impulsive? If that's the case, why not write 'Considered' in the Strengths column? If one of the 'bad' points is that it is pedantic, then surely a strength must be that it is thorough? Now you're getting the picture!

You may have wondered why 'Habits' was in the Weaknesses column. Well, we all have them – and we're not talking about illegal substances in this instance, although addiction is touched upon in parts. Some people live their life by habit, some have relatively few; the problem with habits is that they can become invisible chains. 'I can't go to that party, I always do my mum's shopping on a Thursday evening.' Sound familiar? It may be a good thing that you 'always do' but, occasionally, do something different! Maybe what you 'always *do*' is holding you back from who you might *be*.

Also, an understanding of our habits can help us find situations in which we will thrive, and help us to avoid situations in which we will experience too much stress or temptation. For example, you may think you are drinking too much, in which case you can take the decision to spend less habitual time indulging your habits – 'I always have a glass of wine when I get in from work and, oops, there's the bottle gone'. Why not experiment with drinking tea or half bottles, or do something that brings you home later?

Emotional Intelligence development involves changing attitudes and habits as well as developing new skills and new habits. Therapists say that something becomes a habit after it has been done 21 times, so acquiring a new, good habit should only take three weeks if you do it every day.

You should now have several sheets of paper and two completed columns. You're starting to build up a good picture of what this You is all about, what it can and can't do – maybe – and you're starting to feel quite excited because the You has a longer list of strengths than weaknesses, maybe it's worth something in the marketplace after all! So, now, given its good and not so good points, let's look at what the market is like and how the You fits into it. We're ready to fill in our third column:

Strengths	Weaknesses	Opportunities		
Kind	Obstinate	Promotion		
Loyal	Dithery	Hobby		
Funny	Pedantic	Moving		
Intelligent	Habits	New habits		

Opportunities

There are opportunities in most situations; it mainly depends on how you look at them. Let's say that your company is being taken over by another one. Now that could be a tricky and uncertain time to launch a new product, the YOU into the marketplace. However, it might be just the right time to strike, as the new company isn't familiar with the You and has no negative pre-conceptions about it. With a little tweaking, the You might be just what the newly-formed company needs to fill a skills gap. Do you see what we mean? It's how you look at a situation that determines the outcome, not the situation itself. Or, maybe the You has outgrown a market – come to the end of its natural life within one. While it is normal to mourn the passing of any long-term arrangement, it also usually heralds the beginning of a new one, which might be altogether better. Let's say that the You has always been produced in Kettering; might it not be better received in this day and age in Manchester? Are there more opportunities in Manchester for the special strengths and attributes the You possesses?

Look at the situation the You finds itself in from all angles and write down every opportunity in the third column. Use the Strengths column to help you do this. For example, if you have written 'Creative' in the first column and there is potentially a new opening in the marketing department for the You, then an opportunity could be a new job or change of career. And what about the 'New Habits' entry? Could there be a development class for the You coming up? It might be a physical attribute you would like to develop or something more abstract but any improvement would be a great new habit to acquire.

Actually, if you really think about it, you could virtually write anything realistic – and we use the term loosely – in the Opportunities column, as most of the reasons you will find for not writing one down are merely self-imposed perceptions. Our advice is, if an opportunity pops into your head – and they will, if you open your mind and follow your instincts for this exercise – and if quick as a flash you immediately think 'Oh, no, that's not suitable', ask yourself why. You'll come up with all sorts of excuses (disguised as reasons) why this should be so but if you pull every 'reason' apart you will usually find that it is a miserable little excuse at its heart. If you want to live your life lurching from excuse to excuse, feel free, but you're not really doing your best for the YOU, are you? And that's what you're supposed to be here for...

Sorry, we've given you quite a hard time with all this talk of excuses and bad habits and how you can do anything in the world you want if you just set your mind to it. Please don't feel small or beaten just because you haven't entered the marathon dressed as a juggling Morris Dancer. Throughout this book we are trying to be realistic. Yes, there are amazing people out there who have overcome incredible difficulties to accomplish eye-watering things but they're probably not our audience, not for this book. Everything starts with baby steps, so all we're doing here are the basics. We have written other books on how to achieve anything you want out of life but this one is about Emotional Intelligence and we're in the middle of self-awareness, so we'll stop digressing!

What we're trying to say is that in most people's lives there are a fair few obstacles, which look impossible to overcome; what we're going to address here is how that can be done. So, we go back to our grid:

Strengths	Weaknesses	Opportunities	Obstacles	
Kind	Obstinate	Promotion	Money	
Loyal	Dithery	Hobby	Time	
Funny	Pedantic	Moving	Other people	
Intelligent	Habits	New habits	Habits	

Obstacles

So, we're back to the reasons/excuses why the You shouldn't be in such and such a market. Let's say that you have decided that the You needs to streamline its shape – a lot of Yous have this problem. The main reasons/excuses for not succeeding in this area are listed above:

- 'Without money, I can't take the You to the gym'. (Walking is free, we say, reasonably).
- 'I don't have time to go for a power walk'. (What soaps do you watch when you could be out for a walk?)
- 'My husband/wife/child/parent/friend needs sandwiches making/the shopping done/clean, ironed clothes'. (Would they prefer this done or a happy You round the house?)

- 'I would follow this diet but we always have chips on a Friday.' (Let everyone else have chips and you have salad – they'll still sit with you and love you).
- Or, the big one, 'What would Tom/Dick/Harry think if I did that? It doesn't matter what anyone else thinks, we cry! It's your life.

You see we're back to excuses. Now we're not saying that there are no such things as obstacles; what we're saying is that some obstacles really are miserable little excuses, which can be kicked aside as you stride down your path. Other obstacles really are that – things that get in the way and which are too big and too scary to kick aside. *So, go round them.*

Let's say that you really want to get a new job but haven't got the IT skills/qualification you need. You could go on a course to gain these. 'Right,' you say, 'that's all very well but I haven't got the money'. Then work part-time in the evenings to get the money or see if you fit into any of the many subsidized groups of people, who qualify for help with adult learning.

We could give you many examples of people who have worked at two or even three jobs to achieve their goals – and had families and other responsibilities at the same time. Just make that distinction – is it a real obstacle or is it a miserable little excuse? Either can be overcome with imagination and determination.

Almost there now with our grid and you should be feeling fantastic, as you look at your You. It has so many more strong features than flaws and the opportunities for it in the marketplace are beckoning; you've identified how to overcome any real obstacles there may be for the You to achieve its full potential and now all you have to do is launch it. But, hang on, wasn't the chapter entitled SWOON? Surely we've only got to SWOO to achieve our aims? Not quite – what we haven't addressed is why we want to do any of this anyway.

What do we need to get out of this exercise? What flicks our switch? What makes us happy – really happy? To find out, let's fill in the last column of our grid:

Strengths	Weaknesses	Opportunities	Obstacles	Needs
Kind	Obstinate	Promotion	Money	Praise
Loyal	Dithery	Hobby	Time	Financial security
Funny	Pedantic	Moving	Other people	Approval
Intelligent	Habits	New habits	Habits	Emotional security

Needs

Behavioural psychologists such as Maslow and Herzberg have identified a variety of psychological needs that drive our behaviours, such as the needs for esteem, affection, respect, belonging, achievement, self-actualisation, power and control. What does your You need to shine? Although you might think that this column should have come first, as it is the driving force in designing the You, in reality it can't, as it is the hardest column to fill in, particularly honestly. To admit that one is motivated by money doesn't seem very edifying. However, if that really is your driving force, then admit it and work towards fulfilling that need; anything else would make you dishonest in your life, which is the opposite of Emotional Intelligence. Needs cause motivation; and when they aren't satisfied, they can cause frustration, conflict and stress. Without looking at your strengths and weaknesses you can't begin to understand the deeper, motivational needs, which get you out of bed in the morning.

Awareness of your psychological needs can increase your motivation by helping you understand and seek out the rewards that you really desire, such as a sense of accomplishment, additional responsibility, praise or an opportunity to help others. For example, you may not be motivated by money but by praise and acknowledgement, whereas others need to be needed and will work for nothing at all.

It's also important that you know and focus on your own personal values or principles. It can be very easy to lose sight of those priorities on a day-to-day, moment-by-moment basis. During the working day, so many problems and opportunities arise that the 'things to do' list can easily exceed the time we have to do them. Since few (if any) of those things pertain to what we value most, it's easy to spend too much time on lower priority activities. When we focus on our values, we are more likely to accomplish what we consider most important. It's also a truth that many of us are afraid of succeeding, so we put off doing what we know will help us to achieve success. In fact, we often subconsciously sabotage our own efforts. Does that sound mad? Just think about how often you've done it. We'll explore this in more depth later on.

However, now you have completed your SWOON chart you will be able to write out your own action plan of what you need to do to make those changes; you will be able to build on your strengths, be aware of your weaknesses, make the most of your opportunities and maybe view your perceived obstacles from a different angle.

There are lots of exercises, such as the above, to help identify your strength and weaknesses. However, as the quote from Jung observes, it can be a scary experience holding up a mirror to the deepest parts of yourself. Goethe put it beautifully:

'Know thyself? If I knew myself, I would run away.'

We know how he feels! But, if we pluck up our courage and

really develop our awareness of ourselves, we can only benefit. Self-awareness helps you to maximise your strengths and cope with your weaknesses or vulnerabilities. For instance, you may be kind or thoughtful but also easily-led, which, if you are aware of it, means you can avoid situations where your kindness could be exploited. Or, you might be the sort of person who falls in love at the drop of a hat. Is that clouding your judgment or obscuring your intuition when dealing with the object of your affections?

People with well-developed emotional self-awareness are more effective intuitive decision makers. In complex situations, intuitive decision makers process large amounts of sometimes unstructured and ambiguous data and they often choose a course of action based on a gut feeling or a sense of what's best. People who are highly and emotionally self-aware are better able to read their gut feelings and use them as aids in their decision making process.

This is why we say that your instincts will become stronger as you develop your EI – just make sure you don't ignore them.

Very self-aware people are also often very good leaders. When we understand what motivates us, what gets us excited and why we behave the way we do, we also have insight into what makes others tick.

To the extent that other people are like you (and of course, there are limits to the similarity), knowing how to motivate yourself is tantamount to knowing how to motivate others.

It's very difficult to cope with poor results when you don't understand what causes them. When you don't know what motivates you and which behaviours to change to improve your performance, you just feel helpless and out of control. Self-awareness is empowering because it can reveal what motivates You – which might not be what motivates someone else.

Emotional Hijack

We have given emotional hijack its own heading, as it is often when emotions are running too high for rational thought that situations go badly wrong and if you can prevent one serious emotional hijack in the course of your life after reading this book then you will have achieved a great deal. We keep saying that we are hoping to achieve balance and with emotional hijack, we have a situation where balance is sadly lacking. Emotional Hijack occurs when a person doesn't know him or herself sufficiently to avoid the flashpoints, which manifest in all of us throughout our lives. If you've never totally 'lost it' count yourself lucky. If you have, you won't want to let it happen again.

If you're not aware of your emotional responses and, more to the point, you feel that They are in control of You, then you are in danger of being overtaken by Emotional Hijack. And when you are in highly emotionally aroused state – in a towering rage, or depressed, for example – it is nearly impossible to call in your <u>rational</u> response before acting or speaking.

Sometimes this kind of immediate, emotional reaction can save our lives. If a lion jumps out at us while we're on safari, we don't want to waste time thinking, 'Wow, it's a lion!' More frequently in the modern world however, instinctive emotional response leads us to say something harmful, to escalate the situation, or even to violence.

To minimize the damage from hijacking, it is important to practise patterns, which lead to de-escalation. From that hijacked state, that condition where your brain is flooded with electro-chemicals, you still have options. You do not need to stay hijacked – you still can choose how you behave. After all, it's only a chemical response and those old adage of closing your eyes and counting to ten really does work.

As we have pointed out when discussing the core emotions, Pre-historic programming determines that we react very quickly to danger:

DANGER..............No   time   to think...............ACT................... ACT NOW!

Our instinctive, pre-historic response to a life-threatening situation is fight, flight or freeze and you have less than 1/1000 of a second to change this response. Your body must act quickly. Of course, today the dangers which precipitate that much reaction are very different to prehistoric times – there are no sabre-toothed tigers at large in today's world!

However, as we explained earlier, the brain reacts violently to potential loss, even if this loss is only perceived (and we use the word 'only' ironically; it is just that most people don't understand that their perception *is* their reality). Thousands of years of practice have refined our ability to protect ourselves from threat and danger. We don't have shells or quills or fangs – we have super-sensitive brains.

What happens in such situations is that your brain tries to find an emotional match (feeling) for your experience, so even a non life-threatening event like personal criticism (which may question your sense of identity) can feel like a threat to life. Let's take the analogy of the song *Delilah*. The story is that the singer has been having a relationship with Delilah and finds out that she has been cheating on him. That is bad enough to threaten his sense of identity as a man, but worse, she laughs in his face when he confronts her, so, as he said, he *'felt the knife in my hand and she laughed no more'*.

This may be an extreme example but it exactly follows the pre-historic response to a perceived threat – except that in this instance the threat isn't the loss of a limb from a wild animal but the loss of a partner, the loss of his sense of masculinity or identity and the loss of his pride. Delilah's laughter is what finally 'pushes his buttons to make him use the knife. As Goleman says in his book Emotional Intelligence:

'The hijacking occurs in an instant, triggering this reaction crucial

moments before the …thinking brain has had a chance to glimpse fully what is happening, let alone decide if it is a good idea.

The hallmark of such a hijack is that once the moment passes, those so possessed have the sense of not knowing what came over them.'

As we have said, this is an extreme reaction but whether you have been pushed in front of at the post office, found out that your partner has cheated on you or been unfairly accused by someone, your brain will look for the nearest pattern that matches those emotions.

So, for example, if someone suddenly shouts at you, you may match to your 'I am under attack' pattern and respond with racing heart, sweaty palms and knots in the gut and the simplistic, pre-historic emotional thinking that goes with it; and all this without being in any real danger. And then, how often have you, in the heat of such a moment, said or done something that afterwards, when you calmed down, you dearly wish you had not? This is what the book is all about – achieving the balance and not being prey to the seesaw.

How, then, do we prevent emotional hijack from happening? If you know how (and that's a big if), you may be able to reason about the situation. So, if someone criticises you, you may feel anxious or angry, but you pause before saying or doing anything and consider a number of possible explanations and responses, looking for the one that will be most beneficial overall, rather than coming straight out with your emotional response. Wouldn't that be a wonderful skill to learn?

In the pre emotional hijack stage, as mentioned earlier, the biochemicals such as adrenaline are just beginning to kick in and there is still some wriggle room to use stress management techniques and to listen to the signals coming from your body in order to manage the fight, flight or freeze response more effectively.

At this stage self-awareness is critical because this is what enables you to understand what your body is saying to you. If you pick up these messages you will be able to buy some time to keep the 'biochemical soup ' from becoming too concentrated. At this point there are various strategies you can use to diffuse this potential hijack. For example, you could:

- Count to 10
- Ask someone else for help
- Visualize potential outcomes
- Use humour
- Breathe deeply from your diaphragm, as it will relax you. Take at least six breaths

These strategies sound good, don't they? The only problem is that in this sort of situation, we're usually also dealing with another person, who has their own super-sensitive brain detecting threats; they also have their needs and motivations and they may have, quite simply, 'got out of bed on the wrong side'. What do you do then?

Going back to the pre-historic brain, the core emotions have now been aroused in two people – you and your 'aggressor'. You will both instinctively either 'fight, flee or freeze'. It is almost impossible to avoid that impulse. We are literally hard-wired to react in that way to defend ourselves against threats. You will be defensive by attacking back, retreating, evading, or being externally passive. Of course, depending on your reaction, you can almost guarantee that your 'aggressor' will respond with one of those as well and then the situation escalates. These reactions are actually examples of the intelligence of our emotions – a kind of emotional logic is followed and decisions are made with little or no cognitive thought; the problem is that few of us have developed this aspect of our intelligence.

Think how often something like this happens to you: You think you're acting calmly, but people respond as if you've attacked them. One reason for this response comes from another survival mechanism in our limbic (emotional) brains. Not only do we act to protect ourselves when we are attacked, we are also keenly sensitive to potential threats. The limbic brain actually seeks out feelings in others that indicate danger – it's like a 'Danger Radar'. A danger radar facility looks for potentially hostile emotions, such as anger, frustration, fear and anxiety. Anxiety is a major issue in today's stressful environment – our brains are constantly alerting us to be prepared for battle.

When you are talking, unbeknown to your conscious self, your limbic brain is operating as danger radar checking the whole environment out. Let's say I am trying to appear calm, but underneath I'm really wound up. Not with you, I 'm just frustrated about something I heard or read earlier. So I talk to you, and ask you to do something for me. My words, to me, are not unreasonable (nor would they be to you, in another situation), but underneath, your radar is picking something else up. You are sensing that my words and my feelings don't match. You might not know exactly *what* I'm feeling; yet you simply sense there's an issue underneath. Just this mismatch itself is enough to create fear or anxiety in you – after all, I 'm hiding something from you, and your limbic brain knows that when people are deceiving you, it might be because they want to hurt you. Fiendish thing, the brain!

One way our Danger Radar works is by reading facial expressions and tone of voice. That's why we said that my words could be classed as entirely innocent if not said by me, to you, at that time and in that way. Most researchers agree that only 7% of communication is understood via spoken words (aural) – the rest is sound, tone, body language, and expression.

Research work on facial expression reinforces this conclusion; it has been found that people display a massive amount of emotional information through micro expressions that constantly flit across all our faces and bodies. While most people notice general patterns of these expressions, very few can accurately read a stream of micro expressions. So, while we can tell in general that someone is irritated, angry or upset, and trying to hide something, we probably can't tell if those emotions are directed at us!

In any case, in the midst of our interaction, there is a lot of room for underlying emotions and intentions to influence our thinking. Plus, to add to the mix, we both inhabit our own version of the reality of the moment. You might not know exactly what's going on with me, but you sense a lack of congruence or authenticity. You hear the words I'm saying but they don't match with what my body is saying. Depending on your feelings and experience, and our relationship, your limbic brain sends you to battle stations, and then we can become reactive to one another very quickly. Given this dynamic, it's no wonder people spend so much time and energy attacking and defending, being right and making others wrong. Achieving balance is so difficult in this maelstrom of emotional reactions.

As we've demonstrated, emotion is powerful and we can choose to use that power advantageously or to conflict with it. How then, in the midst of the stresses and strains of daily life, do we use our emotions as a source of power and then effortlessly sail through such confrontation? The challenge is to discover the effortlessness; the opposite of defence by attack. Some people call it surrender, some call it peace, and some call it being in 'the zone'.

Simply accepting that we *can* experience emotion is a big step to achieving 'the zone'. It helps us to see the polarities of choice, so that while we are in the moment we can know what we are choosing: We can let emotion flow and change, or we can be stuck in one emotion, constantly re-creating the same feelings and acting out the same old patterns. We can experience emotions in a smooth way, dealing with each one as it comes, or we can put them aside until they pop out unannounced – to be avoided wherever possible. We can let emotion flow gently, or we can use it like a weapon.

Quick exercise - Danger Radar

It is recommended that you invest time in becoming more aware of the Danger Radar we mentioned earlier. Danger Radars are particularly sensitive to a fear of losing power. If people feel a sense of helplessness, of fear, or loss of control, they may feel very uncomfortable. In those moments, they may feel compelled to show (themselves, mostly) that they are not helpless. They try to exert power over another by being right, or by showing they have the answer, or by dismissing the others' point of view. It could be being more right than their colleagues, friends, boss, children, partner or a parent. It follows the best form of defence is attack school of thought.

For the next day or two, keep a note of when you either get angry, frustrated, afraid, or defensive. Don't re-live the argument/confrontation/trigger, just make notes in your Emotional Journal.

- Can you identify the trigger(s)?
- What other feelings do you have at the same time?
- When do you find yourself wanting to fight?
- To flee?
- To freeze, withdraw or to shut down?
- What physical sensations do you have at these times and where are they? Are they in your palms, fingers, limbs, face, gut, or your neck/back/shoulders – or somewhere else entirely?

Keep a diary of these occasions and jot down the feelings you have and where you have them. When you know that certain actions or words get your guts to knot up, for example, you are well down the path of being self-aware. This should mean that when your Danger Radar 'pings' in a potential emotional hijack situation, you can use one of the stalling tactics we've mentioned.

If, however, you were unable to prevent being emotionally hijacked and your brain has become flooded with emotional charges, it is important to take at least 20 minutes to calm down before starting on any negotiation, reparation or other activities.

Also, as with any other form of stress, physical activity helps to calm a person down. The old adage of 'taking a walk round the block' works both physically and figuratively. Do whatever you do to blow off steam. And don't beat yourself up (if you'll pardon the pun!) for losing your temper, or whatever it was you said or did. At least you're *trying* to harmonise your emotional reaction with your rational thought and you 'll succeed next time. And if you get constantly worked up by something you have no power to change, like next door 's dog barking its head off at 6.00am, just remember these words:

'God, grant me the serenity to accept the things I cannot change; the courage to change the things I can and the wisdom to know the difference' Reinhold Niebuhr

In other words, work at what you can change and accept what you can't without worrying about it.

Chapter Four

Emotional Literacy

How Is Your Emotional Vocabulary?

Do you have a good emotional vocabulary? What are you feeling right now? Write it down here:

What did you write down? Bored, disappointed, anxious, exhilarated (that would be nice!), amused, depressed? As you carry on reading, just test your emotions at random and jot down what you 're feeling in your EI journal. In your quiet moments it can be interesting to just stop and take your emotional pulse now and again. And look for synonyms or 'shades' of words. For example, do you feel happy or content? Did you like the cabbage you had for lunch, love it or adore it?

Now that we're unashamedly navel-gazing, let's explain why this is important and not just a self-indulgent exercise of the terminally bored.

Apart from being self-aware and honest with ourselves, being able to put a name to the emotions raging round inside us is to be able to precisely identify and communicate our feelings. We must communicate our feelings in order to get the emotional support and understanding we need *from* others, as well as to show our emotional support and understanding *to* them.

If you're not used to talking about your feelings – and we 've already agreed that it's not 'normal' – a good place to start is with simple, three word sentences such as these:

I feel sad.

I feel excited.

I feel upset.

I feel lustful.

I feel hurt.

I feel miserable.

And just think for a moment why we say that we *feel* emotions and *think* thoughts. If you think about it logically, you can't feel a thought (you might be able to see one but that's in another book!). By the same token, neither can you think a feeling, apart from in the abstract and that won't get you very far in your pursuit of Emotional Intelligence. Quite often, people with high IQs use 'think' where they should use 'feel' because they are out of balance. They are not used to the messy, 'squiggly' nature of emotions; they prefer the clean, straight lines of thought. So, if you're one of them, start using 'feel' more. It might have the following effect.

Sometimes just by naming a feeling, we begin to actually feel the feeling. It is as if by naming it we give the thinking brain permission to access its emotional part.

This step of identifying the feeling by name is essential to the development of one's innate emotional processing abilities. It can be quite scary for the sort of person we were just describing because once you let that old guard down, emotions can fly in from all angles and envelop you in their messiness. Don't worry though, once you get used to it, just like eventually diving into a warm pool after faffing about at the edge for ages, you'll just love it!

Here, then, are a few basic feeling words to practice with:

Happy	Unhappy, sad
Secure	Insecure, nervous

Peaceful	Anxious, tense
Confident	Scared
Encouraged	Discouraged

Apart from expressing a feeling accurately, these words can also express the intensity of the feeling. By expressing intensity, they communicate the degree to which our needs are being (or not being) met and our values and beliefs are being upheld. Accurately capturing the intensity of an emotion is critical to judging the message our feelings are sending. If we either exaggerate or minimise the feeling, we are distorting reality and undermining the effectiveness of our communication. There are several common ways to verbally express the intensity of a feeling, as shown below:

- Weighting the feeling with a modifier.
  "I feel a little bit disappointed" as opposed to "I feel extremely disappointed."

- Choosing a specific word on the continuum of that emotion.
  "I feel: anxious... angry ... incensed..."

- Making use of the familiar 0 to 10 scale. "On a happy scale of 1 to 10, I feel about an 8."

However, generally speaking, we just aren't taught to use feeling words. Maybe this is because, as a society, we aren't encouraged to share feelings or it may be because to accurately show our feelings makes us feel too vulnerable or 'naked'. Or, we may fear that the person who asks us how we are doesn't really want to know the answer – or maybe we feel that we're not worthy of their notice? We will examine emotional dishonesty later but just consider how often, when you're feeling miserable, sad or unsupported, do you answer "fine" to the question "How are you?"

When we talk about our feelings using three words sentences we are sending what have been called 'I messages'. It's logical when you think about it. "I felt disappointed" when such and such happened" puts the speaker – the 'I' in control. On the other hand when we say things like "You made me so jealous" we are sending a 'you' message. These 'you' messages typically put the other person on the defensive, which hurts communication and relationships rather than helping. It also takes the control – and therefore the responsibility – away from the speaker and makes him or her the 'victim'. Some people use this technique a lot to manipulate others. Look out for it and jot occurrences of it down in your emotional journal.

Remember what we said about the only person who is in control of you is you? If you push the responsibility for an action onto the other person, then you aren't taking control and you can't be free. For example, if you're having a row with your partner and you say "when you did so and so, you made me feel so angry", what you <u>mean</u> is that you chose to be angered by your partner's action. You could have chosen to be amused, scornful or bewildered but you're implying that you had no say in the matter and were forced to be angry. Feel angry by all means but have the courage to acknowledge that it is *your* choice. Take the responsibility. Own the emotion. Note down these occurrences too and you will soon build up a picture of whether you are in control or allowing others to control you.

The ability to identify and name feelings is a form of power, and like all power it can be used to hurt or help. Also, we have a natural fear of the unknown, which is removed when the feelings are named. When we label our feeling, we move it from the unknown to the known and thus we help make it less scary and more manageable. Naming the other person's feeling seems to have a disarming or a de-masking value too and makes clear communication easier.

Also, to get technical, when we label something, we are using a different part of the brain from where we feel the feeling. We are actually diffusing and moving the chemicals from their concentration in the emotional section to the cognitive section, where the pain is not felt as much. Naming a feeling can be used as a form of counter-attack, or it can be used as a form of understanding and agreement. It all depends on how the technique is used. By beginning to think about our feeling, we are also taking the next step towards solving our problem. When our thoughts are clear, this helps us feel more in control and empowered.

How often have you said one thing and meant another, or had your words twisted by your listener? Sometimes, this mis-communication just boils down to a lack of practice. Sometimes, however, we hide behind labels – listen to any young person today and count the number of 'like' references. You'll give up after the first 20… What these people don't realize is that they are hiding what they actually want to say and are almost at the stage of 'thinking' their feelings.

In the examples below we are labelling ourselves, and not clearly and directly expressing our feelings. *'I feel like: … a clown … a baby … a moron.'*

These statements are quite graphic, as they convey a picture in a word, but they are generally expressions which put ourselves down. These negative labels certainly don't help us feel any better about ourselves. In fact, by mentally branding us, they make it more likely we will repeat the exact kinds of actions which caused our feelings in the first place.

In the following examples we are actually conveying more of a thought than a feeling.

'I feel like you're a nutter.' 'I felt like it was weird.' 'I feel like she's going to win.'

We can also express our feelings in the form of a behaviour.

Again, these are unclear and indirect. They may also be graphic and entertaining, but they are usually exaggerations and distortions, which don't help us focus on our true feelings.

'I feel like: ... strangling him' ... *'shooting him'* ... *'wringing his neck'...* *'teaching her a lesson'* ... *'punching him'* ... *'dumping her'* ... *'throwing myself off a cliff'.*

In other words, people who use such expressions feel like behaviour, an action or an act. Thus, they may not be in touch with their feelings. They may be acting out their lives as they think others would, rather than acting as unique individuals. Or they simply imagine themselves taking action rather than actually using their emotions to motivate them to take the appropriate action.

Like anything else, the more we practise identifying emotions, the better we get at quickly selecting the correct name for the feeling. Each time we identify an emotion and assign a label to it, the brain's cognitive and emotional systems work together to remember the emotion, the circumstances and the label for the emotion. This is Emotional Literacy. This is where your Emotional Journal helps.

After we learn to find the right words and intensity of them for our feelings and get into the habit of being accurate in how we express them, the next step is explaining why we feel what we feel.

At this point, our analytical brain is called into action. We actually make things much easier for ourselves and others when our language is clear, direct, and precise. When our words and our non-verbal communication are consistent with each other, we gain respect because we come across as having integrity. Clear, honest communication is not only helpful in personal relationships, but is essential to a society. We are simply all better off when we all follow the old rule:

Say what you mean and mean what you say.

Chapter Five

Acceptance and Understanding of Emotions

Acceptance

'We cannot change anything unless we accept it. Condemnation does not liberate, it oppresses.'
Jung

You may have heard that some emotions are positive and some are negative. That isn't necessarily true. Fear, for example, may be considered a negative emotion but fear put to work can achieve great results – you escape your lion at any rate! Plus, as we learned in the emotional literacy section, these are just the labels we give emotions and all emotions are valid. It may just be that we prefer not to experience some of the less pleasant ones at the expense of the nicer ones. As Daniel Goleman says, every feeling has its value and significance.

Love, fear, anger, disgust, compassion et al all flicker through us all the time evoking distinct feelings and emotions. In reality, though, there is no difference between any of them. They are all manifestations or facets of an aspect of ourselves, like the ocean of earlier, which we exaggerate or suppress depending on the circumstances. Often, it is the fluctuating energy level that is responsible for varying physical and mental states—unless, that is, you are in total control over your mind and body (in which case, you'd be unlikely to be reading this!).

We've all experienced how some days we feel that no job is too big or too difficult, life is a breeze and we can cope with almost anything it throws at us. Then, there are those days when even getting out of bed in the morning is too much. The world seems to conspire behind your back and anything that can go wrong, does. Sod's Law rules! If only it were possible to crawl into a hole and forget the day started.

The skill lies in **recognizing**, which we have already done and **accepting** one's emotions.

As we have discussed, we instinctively strive to envelop ourselves in the so-called 'good' emotions like love, compassion, elation and contentment, while negating or suppressing the 'bad' ones like anger, fear, lust and abhorrence. This is a mistake, as 'bad' emotions are only symptoms of blocks in the body or the lack of 'flow' we have achieved.

Ignoring or suppressing these blocks does not cause them to vanish; what is more likely to happen is the strengthening of the blocks and problems later in life, which we touched on in the Inner Child. Also, without the downs we can't appreciate the ups. Never allowing oneself to experience anger, for example, is not healthy. Experiencing it on a daily basis however is equally inappropriate. The key is to have a healthy balance of both.

Energy, like the water in a fountain, must be allowed to flow — keeping it bottled up <u>will</u> result in spillage. If we suppress emotions, one day they will jump out and bite us, often in a magnified way, when we least expect it. There is a harrowing story told by Elizabeth Kübler-Ross, which tells of her very strict upbringing by a harsh (we would say sadistic) father. As a child, Elizabeth had a pet rabbit, which was kept with the rabbits for the pot. One Sunday, when choosing the rabbit to be killed, cooked and eaten, Elizabeth's father deliberately pointed to her pet for execution. Not only did he then kill it, but he forced her to take the still-warm body to the kitchen and then later eat the result. The poor child wasn't even allowed to comment, let alone cry.

Many years later, as a successful, professional adult, Elizabeth was at Customs in an airport. When the Customs officer pointed at her suitcase, presumably with an emotionless face, as they are trained to have, Elizabeth was suddenly overwhelmed by the same emotions she had experienced on that Sunday so many years before and, to put it colloquially, totally 'lost it'. It was the first time she had accepted the feelings and allowed them an outing, even though she would never have done so publicly without the trigger.

The first step in accepting and managing feelings is to break down the classification of good and bad emotions. For instance, consider a situation when you are moved to tears by a particularly touching scene in a film or a book. What happens is that the situation you are reading about or viewing touches your heart, thereby permitting a free flow of energy and yet it is sufficiently divorced from the self to be 'allowable'.

The emotion you experience is a result of this rush of energy, which had been lying dormant. If you have undergone similar experiences with a so-called negative emotion like disgust, hatred or anger, count yourself blessed, as you can learn so much from it. And if you haven't, try opening yourself to the emotion the next time it occurs until you feel yourself totally enveloped in it – however painful it might be. The experience can be as enriching and fulfilling as a rush of good emotion. Don't get us wrong, we are not advocating loss of self-control and wallowing in emotion until you can attribute all responsibility for your actions to that emotion.

Just as you let yourself go while watching a film or reading a book, while maintaining awareness of your real self, be aware of yourself and then let the emotions wash over you. With practice you will be able to view past events dispassionately and use the experiences and feelings as they building blocks to a better self. It may not seem so while experiencing them, but harrowing feelings really can be beneficial after time.

Initially, you may have to consciously make yourself aware of situations in which you are letting your feelings collect inside you, and then make an effort to experience them. With time this will become spontaneous and the experience will become easier, until you feel every little emotion while retaining complete awareness of it. That does not mean that you have to walk around wearing your emotions like a badge on your chest. It just means that while trying to hide your emotions from the world, you don 't end up hiding them from yourself too.

Let's take grief. Going through grief is not a pleasant experience by any stretch of the imagination but, when grief is the appropriate response, denying the emotion, pushing it in a box and shutting the lid will store up all sorts of 'nasties' for the future. How many times have you been urged to 'get something off your chest'? Allow yourself to feel it and acknowledge that it is a valid and appropriate response. Maybe you've been dumped by a partner, maybe a close friend or family member has died; whatever the situation that causes you grief, being present in the emotion is the best way forward – it just doesn't feel it at the time. But, be aware that if you don't deal with it now – even if 'dealing' with it only consists of acknowledging it, it will surely come back doubled or trebled at some point in the future.

Visualize yourself in the same situations again, and this time, permit yourself to experience the moods and feelings that you had shut out earlier. Cry if you want to, or laugh, scream or get angry; just try and do it in a safe environment, where you can 't do yourself – or anyone else – any harm. At the end, thank yourself for removing the power those pent-up feelings would have had over you if you hadn't let them take their natural course. Ignoring your emotions just won't work because one day they will come back to haunt you and the response to something seemingly trivial could be totally out of proportion to the event itself and you could find yourself at the mercy of Emotional Hijack.

Self-Esteem

The dictionary definition of self-esteem is *'a person's self-appraisal of their own worth.'*

So, on a scale of 1 – 10, how much do YOU feel you are worth?

Write down the number on the scale in your Emotional Journal, date it and keep going back to your scores. They will get higher, as you keep developing. Self-esteem may be expressed as an overall generic characteristic, for example, 'she exhibits a high self-esteem' or 'she has a strong sense of her own self-worth'. Sometimes, it is a more specific behavioural attribute, such as 'he knows he's a superb footballer but feels an idiot in the classroom.'

Interestingly, Daniel Goleman doesn't talk much about self-esteem in his book. He refers more to optimistic or pessimistic people, which we will discuss later. It is hard to understand, however, how a self-aware person cannot know the level of his or her self-esteem. And how confident a person is in their own worth is so important.

Most people's feelings and thoughts about themselves fluctuate somewhat based on their daily experiences. The mark you get in an exam, how your friends treat you, the ups and downs in a romantic relationship can all have a temporary impact on your wellbeing. Your self-esteem, however, is something more fundamental than the normal ups and downs associated with situational changes. For people with good basic self-esteem, normal ups and downs may lead to temporary fluctuations in how they feel about themselves, but only to a limited extent and they can generally take whatever curved balls life throw at them. In contrast, for people with poor basic self-esteem, these ups and downs may make all the difference in the world and can even be the trigger that sends a person over the edge.

Our self-esteem develops and evolves throughout our lives, as we build an image of ourselves through our experiences with different people and activities. Experiences during our childhood play a particularly large role in the shaping of our basic self-esteem. (Remember the Inner Child). When we were growing up, our successes (and failures) and how the members of our immediate family or teachers and peers treated us, all contributed to the creation of our basic self-esteem.

Our past experiences, even the things we don't usually think about, are all alive and active in our daily life in the form of a Critical Voice, which we spoke about earlier. Although most people do not hear this voice in the same way they would a spoken one, in many ways it acts in a similar way, constantly repeating those original messages to us.

For people with healthy self-esteem the messages of the critical voice are generally positive and reassuring. For people with low self-esteem, the critical voice becomes a harsh inner critic, constantly criticising, punishing, and belittling their accomplishments. Very often, the phrases used can be traced back to a specific person or people – 'you'll never amount to anything' from a parent or teacher, for example.

One of the aims of the book is to help you boost your self-esteem but, if you are like most people, the chances are you have some issues with your own confidence in yourself. Low self-esteem can have devastating consequences.

- It can create anxiety, stress, loneliness and increased likelihood for depression.
- It can cause problems with friendships and relationships.
- It can seriously impair academic and job performance.
- It can lead to underachievement and increased vulnerability to drug and alcohol abuse.

Worst of all, these negative consequences themselves reinforce the negative self-image and can take a person into a downward spiral of lower and lower self-esteem and increasingly non-productive or even actively self-destructive behaviour.

So, how do we boost our self-esteem? The easiest way is to challenge the Critical Voice. Let's say that you're in a situation with someone and you think:

"He looks angry. He hasn't said anything, but I know it means he

doesn't like me!"

Think about this thought and then pretend you have a friend with you, who could maybe offer this suggestion: *"OK, he looks angry, but you don't know why. It could have nothing to do with you. Maybe you should ask him."*

Another way to boost your self-esteem is to look after yourself – as L'Oréal says, 'because you're worth it!' – and do some things that make you feel good and don't hurt yourself or anyone else. Maybe go for a walk, sit and look at the sunset, watch a favourite film, have a nap or pick on something good about yourself – your good manners, hair, teeth, eyes, and really praise yourself for that one aspect. Even if you don't believe you're worth the praise, it will become natural to you in time – remember the 21 repeats to form a habit. Write down the good things about yourself in your EI journal at least once a week. As you re-read, you will be amazed at how much longer the list gets as time goes on.

Quick exercise – Good Things You Have Done

Get your Emotional Journal out and make a list of what you 've accomplished recently. This could be today, in the last week, month or even few months. If you 've had an on-going hard time, it can be very easy to lose sight of your achievements. They may have been tiny, but remember the baby steps. To have achieved anything when beset with problems is remarkable. Maybe all you did today was put on your make-up or said No. Great. It's a step forward. Praise yourself for what you 've achieved, out loud if practical. And/or send a close friend an email saying how proud you are of yourself and invite them to reciprocate. We're all too often reticent about 'blowing our own trumpet' but it can do us the world of good to remind ourselves of how far we 've come and what we've achieved.

Getting help from others is often the most important step a

person can take to improve his or her self-esteem, but it can also be the most difficult. As we 've just said, people with low self-esteem often don't ask for help because they feel they don 't deserve it. But since low self-esteem is often caused by how other people treated you in the past, you may need the help of other people in the present to challenge the critical messages that come from negative past experiences. Here are some ways to get help from others:

- Ask friends to tell you what they like about you or think you do well.
- Ask someone who cares about you to just listen to you rant for a little while without interrupting, even with positive messages. Get it off your chest!
- Ask for a hug.
- Ask someone who loves you in any way to remind you that they do and why.

Sometimes low self-esteem can feel so painful or difficult to overcome that professional help is needed. Go to a recommended therapist or, if money is an issue, borrow some self-help books from the library and you'll quickly realise that you are not on your own.

In America, the importance placed on good self-esteem is so high that some states have even established commissions to study the effect of self-esteem, and make recommendations promoting this concept. The 'California Task Force to Promote Self-esteem' made the following generalizations:

- People who hold themselves in high esteem are less likely to engage in destructive and self-destructive behaviour, including child abuse, alcohol and drug abuse, violence and crime.
- Young girls who have positive self-esteem are less likely to

become pregnant as teenagers.

- High self-esteem can never be given to a person by another person or society. It must be sought and earned by the individual for him or herself.
- Though the definition of the concept varies, commonly used terms include: security, connectedness, uniqueness, assertiveness, competence and spirituality.

It would appear, then, that anything an individual can do to increase their own self-esteem can only be good for them and everyone around them. Use your journal and chart how well you 're doing and how much you're improving on a daily basis. We will show you some visualisations later in the book to promote your sense of self.

Adaptability and Change

'It is not the strongest of the species who survive, nor the most intelligent but those who are most adaptive to change.' Charles Darwin

'Change is growth' was on a poster in our office for several years and we still haven't found out who said it but it remains one of life's best aphorisms. As we read in the quote by Charles Darwin, it is not necessarily the most intelligent person who prospers; quite often it is the most adaptable. And note that the focus is on YOU again. Circumstances may not change but the way you look at them can. One of the many self-help books doing the rounds at the moment is *'Ask And It Is Given'* by Esther and Jerry Hicks. This is said to be the teachings of an evolved being, or collection of beings, called Abraham. Abraham says, *'If you want things to change to different things, you must think different thoughts. And that simply requires finding unfamiliar ways of approaching familiar subjects.'*

On a more earth-bound level, let's imagine that you are stuck in a pattern of emotional response. It may be that you find it difficult to say No for fear of offending others. So, when asked to do something you would rather not do, or don't have time for, instead of just saying the 'N' word, you grit your teeth, smile as pleasantly as you can and say 'Yes' but the feelings that build up are of resentment (at the asker), failure (because you've failed to say what you really wanted to say) and anxiety (that you may not do whatever it is well enough to please the asker). It may seem a tiny little step – remember baby steps though – but imagine how you will feel when you actually do say 'No' for the first time, even to a small thing. Imagine it, visualise your relief, bask in the triumph and feel your body relax.

Maybe awful things are happening or have happened to you. They may even be things that the average person would find awful, not just a broken nail. Just remember, though, that apart from death, nothing is insurmountable.

Now that's a bold statement but ask anyone who has been through severe trials and come out the other end intact mentally and they will say that their *attitude* to the trials was the most important thing. We talk a lot more about positivity, hope and optimism later in the book and give examples of incredible courage in the face of adversity, so we'll leave it here for now but just remember that big changes, upheavals and general problems may not be the end of your world as you know it.

As Ivy Baker Priest (ex-treasurer of the US and generally fascinating woman) said, *'The world is round and the place which may seem like the end may also be the beginning. Remember, it 's how you look at and think about the situation that counts.'*

Chapter Six

Self-mastery

Being In Control

So, we now know we have emotions, which flow gently and don 't build up to hijack proportions, we can label them correctly and we can talk to ourselves and screen out the Critical Voice.

We are finally ready to be in control of ourselves. In this section, we will practise self-mastery or management and become authentic.

There are many phrases, which encompass the idea of self-mastery – self-management, self-discipline and self-control. The concept of self-control in itself smacks of authority and high standards. Given this framework, it is easy to feel a failure in almost any area of life. If you're overweight, the unspoken criticism is that you don 't have enough self-control to stick to a diet. If you smoke – especially these days – you don't have enough self-control to give up.

According to Goleman, the self-control ability kicks in between two and three years of age. In fact, we often hear of the 'terrible twos', which is when a child has no control over his or her emotions and has the expected tantrum.

As we go through life, this self-control aspect strengthens, so that, hopefully, an adult won't wail and bawl when told they can 't do or have something. However, the word 'hopefully' is used advisedly, as there are many ways of having a tantrum and there are many adults who continue to have them well into old age! They obviously haven't been reading this book!

Self-management or mastery means having the skill to be able to choose the emotions you want to experience, rather than being the victim of whatever emotions occur. It means not letting others 'push your buttons' and possessing the ability to manage your emotional state. Whatever you do though, please don't confuse 'managing' your emotions with burying or 'putting a lid on' them. As we have said more than once, that is a potentially dangerous and futile pastime. The skill in choosing the emotions you want – typically to be able to transform unpleasant, draining emotional states into positive, productive ones – is having the courage to acknowledge and accept your emotions and then to do something about them.

It is the ability to manage moods, respond effectively to stress, situations of ambiguity or crisis. It also relates to the ability to manage relationships with others to achieve mutual benefit, but we will talk more about that under the Communication heading.

When people have low self-management skills they tend to react impulsively in stressful situations, possibly getting overly stressed, angry or upset when facing rapidly changing situations or conflict at work or at home and sometimes responding to problems in a non-constructive manner – which often causes unwanted consequences, such as emotional hijack. We all know people who can turn a drama into a crisis – and don't they wear you out? Do yourself a favour and give them the book as a present – you could even send it anonymously!

Being impulsive can lead to all sorts of problems. As we have asked before, how many times have you done or said something in the heat of the moment that you have really regretted later? However, if you practise self-mastery, these moments will soon become a thing of the past.

Self-mastery / management requires an optimistic attitude and a strong sense of self-determination. What differentiates a self-master from a self-doubter is that the self-master is willing to participate in life and not just be a passive recipient to whatever life throws at them. Sometimes, people who practise self-mastery are accused of being selfish, as they are doing what is best for them and not what is best for everyone else – usually the person doing the complaining. There is a fine line between selfishness and self-mastery but that is where the other components of morality and ethics come in.

In his book Emotional Intelligence, Goleman writes that, *'There is an old-fashioned word for the body of skills that emotional intelligence represents – character - and....the bedrock of character is self-discipline...or self-control.'*

So, not only are we improving emotional intelligence, we are building character, with all the other attributes that entails, such as increasing empathy, real listening, compassion and altruism, all of which we will discuss in more detail later.

Being able to curb impulsive behaviour has all sorts of social benefits, as well as benefits to the individual. As Goleman says, *' the capacity to impose a delay on impulse is at the root of a plethora of efforts, from staying on a diet to pursuing a medical degree.'*

A recent international study showed that those who feel they have the most control over their lives have a 60% lower risk of illness and death in any given year than those who feel helpless. We could write a whole book about how the mind affects the body but that's not the subject here. Just be aware though that in developing your Emotional Intelligence, you are likely to be lengthening your life – or, as the old joke says – it will just feel longer....

Researchers have found that this sense of one's own power is a major reason for optimists being healthier. Conversely, studies revealed that feeling helpless and negative is extremely stressful and can have bad effects on our health.

The first step to achieving self-mastery is to convince yourself that you can do it. That may seem obvious, but in fact the concept of self-mastery has a strange mystique about it. It just seems like something ordinary people are incapable of – failed diets, failure to give up smoking so many times for example. Perhaps that's the reason so few of us believe in it or ever attempt to achieve it. But, logic and common sense would argue that practising self-mastery should be more natural and effortless than spending much of your life as your own worst enemy. It could turn you from a saboteur into a champion. It could even become a habit.

Think of it this way. The word mastery simply means *"the full command or control of a subject."* Therefore, all self-mastery requires is being in charge of yourself – the Chairman of the Board for your life, if you like – consciously choosing for yourself the thoughts and actions that will make you who and what you want to be. Just seize the controls, instead of being pushed and pulled around by outside factors, and your life is back in your own hands.

'Follow that will and that way which experience confirms to be your own.'
Jung

Is achieving self-mastery really all that easy? Well, yes and no. As you'll read a little later on, there are many psychological and behavioural factors that can keep getting in your own way. But, with a little vigilance, you can easily become the master or mistress of your own world.

The first step in achieving self-mastery is to realise that it is you, your inner world, that you must master – not the outside world, as there's nothing you can do to change that and if you persist in trying to you will just wear yourself out.

Most of the stress that people encounter in their daily existence comes from the never-ending struggle to gain control over all of the outside factors in their lives. The problem is, as we've just said, gaining full control over your outer world is virtually impossible.

Self-mastery is not about controlling everything *in* your life. It's about being in charge *of* your life; in charge of your thoughts and actions and in charge of the way you approach, perceive and respond to the outer world. How you look at the outside world is what's important.

'It all depends on how we look at things, and not on how they are themselves.'
Jung

Being in charge of your inner world means to *live in the present moment*. Unfortunately, no one ever fully explains just how to do that. One way is to become a 'Now-ist' – don't worry, it's not a cult! To Now-ists, stress and unhappiness come from allowing your thoughts and actions to be in conflict with who and what you want to be. Only by being true to your own heartfelt goals and desires can you harmonise Mind, Body and Spirit to act as one and achieve true self-mastery.

Being a 'Now-ist' means living in 'the now' and seizing the opportunities and possibilities in each moment. It means fully engaging in and enjoying the process of every action while surrendering thoughts or concern about the outcome. It also means living as a 'human being', not a 'human doing'. Don't just fill up your time with pursuits you do carelessly, revel in every action in every present moment.

Great idea, you may say and all sounding very simple and easy, and it can be. But, most of us have an annoying habit of getting in our own way – being our own saboteurs. Most of us either live in the past or the future. How often have you heard someone say "When I've lost the weight, I'll..." or "When I've got the new job, I'll..." or "I wish I hadn't made that choice in 1983." The problem is that by living anywhere but in the now, you can't change yourself. Our old friend Abraham Maslow said:

'The ability to be in the present moment is a major component of mental wellness.'

The 'Now-ist' concept of living in accord with your own goals and desires has even been proven to promote greater vitality than exercise, super nutrition and deep relaxation exercises. See, we promised you better health as a side-effect! If it seems like 'Now-ism' can help you in virtually every area of your life, it can. That's what self-mastery is all about.

A true self master has the ability to:

- Stay open to feelings, both those that are pleasant and those that are unpleasant.

- Reflectively engage or detach from an emotion depending upon its judged ability to inform or other use.

- Reflectively monitor emotions in relation to oneself and others, such as recognizing how clear, typical, influential or reasonable they are.

- Manage emotion in oneself and others by moderating negative emotions and enhancing pleasant ones, without repressing or exaggerating the information they may convey.

Self masters understand that their life is in their control now, not in the future. Don't live as Ralph Waldo Emerson describes here:

We are always getting ready to live but never living.

The Authentic Self

'To be normal is the ideal aim of the unsuccessful'.
Jung

What is the 'authentic self'? Authentic means real, genuine and honest and you can substitute any of those. Choose which one feels right for you. As we discussed earlier, your authentic self is not proscribed by your job or rôle or any one facet of your personality. Your authentic self is the true, <u>whole</u> you.

Living authentically is when there is total harmony between your inner world and your outer world. But what does that mean? It certainly doesn't mean that you have no more anxieties or problems. You may even have more as you choose to live authentically. The big difference though is that these anxieties and problems won't shake the foundations of your world like they used to. Truth to tell, a lot of people find those who live a truly authentic life a little odd, as they no longer worry about 'normal' stuff. Still, as Jung points out, who wants to be 'normal'?

We all started off with hopes and dreams but, unfortunately for most of us, life and 'normality' then came and got in the way. How many people do you know that are really happy in themselves? For many people, the conflict between the life they want and the life they lead creates constant anxiety, stress and even ill health. You see, what many people do is live the life of the artificial self, the socialized self, the self that they have created to be perceived as 'normal'.

We could give you many examples of people living artificial lives but two of the saddest cases we have seen recently are men in their 50s. In fact, it's interesting to note that men are more prone to mid-life crisis than women and it could well be attributed to the fact that women are generally more naturally emotionally intelligent than men (don't sue – these are generalizations!)

Anyway, these men we have mentioned both suddenly woke up one morning and decided to leave home because they weren't happy. It wasn't until they came to see us that they realized that it wasn't their wives they wanted to change but their lives – or rather, how they lived their lives.

One is a doctor, who had always wanted to be a professional

singer and one is a barrister, who had always wanted to act. Neither had had the courage to pursue their dreams as young men and had lived these artificial lives, with all the trappings of success – big houses, cars, private schools, holidays etc – but no authenticity. They were both heading for breakdowns of one sort or another but then they learned about living an authentic life. One now sings in a choir and went back to his wife while the other one has affairs – wonder if you can guess which one is happier? One of them forgot what Schiller said:

'Keep true to the dreams of your youth.'

When you create a life where the decisions you make and the actions you take are considered, deliberate, and in harmony with what's important to you, you are living an authentic life. As we have just observed, it's not necessarily a life that *others* endorse or think is right for you, but it's a life that you know in your heart is right for you. It may not be a life that has been your habit, or the one that was mapped out for you but it is a life that makes you greet each day like you did as a child. And you can start it at any age.

Unless we're very unusual or naturally very emotionally intelligent, when we're young adults we tend to want to conform, as we believe that that will make us happy. We often do what our parents want us to do or what our partners think is right for us, like our doctor and our barrister. Sometimes then, later in life, we find the courage to do what we really want to do and are then less motivated to do what others want us to do. Sometimes though we feel trapped in a gilded cage – again like our two men. One of them said that he simply couldn't stop doing what he was doing as he had to pay the school fees and considerable maintenance. When we pointed out that he was the one who had instigated the divorce and could always take his children out of their expensive schools, he acted as if we had suggested he should pour petrol over his head and get careless with matches! The social stigma he perceived he would have to endure was worse than being unhappy.

We say perceived because there are no truly objective facts on which to base anything. Everything we see, everything we feel and everything we 'know' is based on our subjective interpretation of the information, which is fed to us by our senses.

Understanding that there is no objective reality, no single truth and that no one person is actually right is hugely liberating – and quite hard to accept at first. We are so brainwashed by our perceptions, as our man was, that we really *believe* that we must do certain things and must lead our lives in such and such a way. Yes, of course society must have rules to protect the vulnerable but no-one decrees that a person must be an accountant or must go to church every Sunday.

Remember that the world in which you live is your world, which has been constructed by your mind in order to make sense of what is going on outside it. Once you can listen to what your inner voice says is the right path for you and act on it, you can be honest with yourself and see your miserable little excuses for what they really are.

Being honest with ourselves seems hard to start with as we probably have years of conditioning to break through, but once we make the leap it is harder still not to be honest. Once we start to be honest with ourselves, we start to be able to trust ourselves, which gives us more confidence in every situation.

You can probably name several brave people who have taken considerable risks in order to lead more authentic lives. Often they will have been vilified for making whatever changes were necessary to do so but that won't upset them, as they are living a life that is true to their purpose, values and dreams. They will have endured the cries of selfish, regret any hurt their actions caused and then moved on. The trick is to find out what your values and dreams are. Good job you did the SWOON exercise!

The people who have changed their lives have thrown off the chains of conformity and truly written their own script.

There's a lovely story about the island fisherman who meets the business consultant. The consultant asks how long it takes the fisherman to catch enough fish to make ends meet. The fisherman replies that it only takes a few hours. "What do you do with the rest of your time?" asks the consultant.

"I sleep late, fish for a while, play with my children, have an afternoon's rest under a coconut tree. In the evenings, I see my friends, have a few beers, play the drums, and sing a few songs..." replies the fisherman.

The consultant advises that, if the fisherman were to work longer hours and catch more fish, he would make more money and eventually end up controlling a huge enterprise.

"How long would that take?" asked the fisherman.

"Oh, ten, maybe twenty years," replied the consultant.

"And after that?" asked the fisherman.

"Well, when your business gets really big, you can start selling shares in your company and make millions!"

"Millions? Really? And after that?" pressed the fisherman.

"After that you 'll be able to retire, move out to a small village by the sea, sleep late every day, spend time with your family, go fishing, take afternoon naps under a coconut tree, and spend relaxing evenings having drinks with friends...."

It may be a funny story, but how many of us live our lives exactly like that? Instead of appreciating what we have NOW and being happy with it, we chase something we may not even want and end up surprised that we 're not happy.

Once you are really clear about what you need and desire and what aligns your outer behaviour with that inner truth, your life will just flow – it really will. When your inner and outer worlds are as one, the pieces all just seem to fit and everything clicks with no pretence or artifice.

When you don 't live an authentic life, however, nothing flows;

you will find yourself exhausted, irritable and unsettled, always chasing the next rainbow but never finding the pot of gold. We all have unique gifts – yes, even you! – and when we follow the dreams we once had to use those gifts we can be truly balanced and happy.

Being authentic also requires courage, as you have to do the SWOON exercise and face your personal truths. You need to examine every facet of yourself – the good, the bad and the downright ugly but, when you do it you will live a life that exceeds your wildest dreams.

Steve Jobs, (who, as an insight into his Inner Child, was adopted and never completed his degree) founder of Apple Mackintosh and CEO of Pixar Films addressed the Stanford University graduates a couple of years ago. What he said in that speech conveys everything we have been saying, so we'll end with his words, as we can't better them. Read and re-read, then live your life as he suggests:

'For the past 33 years, I have looked in the mirror every morning and asked myself: "If today were the last day of my life, would I want to do what I am about to do today?" And whenever the answer has been "No" for too many days in a row, I know I need to change something.

Your time is limited, so don't waste it living someone else's life. Don't be trapped by dogma — which is living with the results of other people 's thinking. Don't let the noise of others' opinions drown out your own inner voice. And most important, have the courage to follow your heart and intuition. They somehow already know what you truly want to become. Everything else is secondary.'

Chapter Seven

Emotions In Others

Recognizing Emotions In Others

So, far, we've concentrated on our internal world, as we have agreed, hopefully, that the only thing we can really change is inside us. Now, however, we are reaching out to others via communication in its many forms. We may not be able to change the external world but we can communicate with it – or at least try to. Hopefully the following pages will help with your communication skills.

The dictionary says that recognising emotions in others is:

- The ability to identify emotions in other people through language, sound, gestures, appearance, and behaviour.

- The ability to use reason to discriminate between accurate and inaccurate, or honest vs. dishonest expressions of feeling.

What a lot of people don't realize, however, is that communication doesn't just depend on what you say. As we said earlier, 7% is verbal, and the rest is made up of how you say it – 38% – and 55% by your body language. It's also often not what you say that influences others; it's what you *don't* say. Anyone who has been in a relationship can testify to the fact that what they want to say is often not communicated, for a host of reasons. As the song Masquerade says so eloquently:

'We tried to talk it over but the words got in the way.'

The signals that you send non-verbally can suggest anything from attitude, understanding, mood or empathy to ethics. The moment you meet someone else, they judge you by what they see and feel. The process takes less than 10 seconds but the impression is often permanent. The signals that you send (and receive) during this first meeting may make or break a sale, or even change your life.

Non Verbal Communication - Body Language

These other forms of communication are called non-verbal communication. Body language is the main non-verbal communicator between people but there are other aspects including tone of voice, eye movement, posture, hand gestures, facial expressions and more, which contribute to the overall interactive view of communication.

When we are in contact with someone it is *impossible* to be not communicating something, even if that something is subconscious. This is why we find good actors so fascinating, as not only are they able to master their own body language for the role, but they can also act the appropriate body language for the characters they are playing. Generally speaking people with higher EQ are better at reading and understanding these non-verbal cues.

However, we're going to ask you to become actors for a while, as it is important to become conscious of our own and others' body language. Like any language, not only do we have to learn to speak it but also to be able to understand it. Let's start with the basics. When we become proficient in body language, we will be able to:

- Accurately assess a person on first impressions – unless they're acting!
- Accurately read the comfort level (or otherwise) of a person
- Establish rapport with a person using reflective body language routines

- Develop empathy – providing effective support, assistance and encouragement

Body language recognition is like any other skill that can be learned. We all instinctively read the signs that individuals or groups normally transmit and through which we react or act in accordance with our own experiences. However, from a professional standpoint, such as in management, body language reading and understanding is as important as any other subject, as it facilitates the connections and empathy that can lead to trust and reliance. These issues should never be treated lightly as they can be used for good or ill, which we will touch on later. In this context, however, body language understanding is a beneficial skill that everyone attempting to improve their Emotional Intelligence should try to master.

Body language is also interlinked with spoken language and a whole pattern of behaviour from a person. Think of politicians – and mimics. Where would Rory Bremner be without his hand chopping movements when he's mimicking Tony Blair emphasising a point?

Some groups have developed a whole range of specific body language which can be very explicit in its meaning and is used to communicate where the use of words may otherwise be difficult or dangerous. Examples of this are mostly in sector or gender groups, such as gay people, people in slavery, prisoners or workers in specific situations, who may have had to evolve a method of communication which doesn't involve speaking, for various reasons.

It is said that indigenous northerners often have very mobile facial expressions, as mill workers had to exaggerate their words in a form of lip reading because the noise in the mills made normal conversation impossible.

Body language is used especially to express or illustrate feelings, emotion and/or attitudes – back to Tony Blair and his emphatic hands. For instance if we do not like someone, it is often difficult to say that directly to the person. However, we can make it clear either intentionally or unintentionally through our body language. Be warned though, as the opposite is also true; if you fancy the bloke in sales and don't want him to know, be very careful not only in what you say but how you act! Remember what Mae West said: *'I speak two languages, Body and English!'*

For example, let's say that we are happy through words. In a relationship, again, we might be telling our partner verbally that we are fine with him/her going away on a college reunion weekend yet our body language may be saying loud and clear that we are not. This can be very confusing for the receiver and is usually described as giving out mixed messages – one message in words and an opposite message in body language. It is also difficult to lie or cover up our feelings through body language, unless we are gifted actors or con men. People may give their true feelings away by not being aware of their body language – you were warned!

Research has shown that most people pay more attention to, and believe more readily, their impression of how a person acts through body language than what is said through words. As a consequence we tend to doubt, or put a question mark behind, the spoken words if they do not correspond with the language of the body. A good example is when a person agrees to something while shaking their head. It also leads to a defensive attitude on the part of the listener, as their danger radar will be pinging madly at this incongruity.

So, we've illustrated that how we come across to someone is decided only in a small part by the words we speak. To leave a good impression behind, say on a first date, it is important that we know, and to a certain extent can control, our body language. The person on the receiving end of our body language will have a feeling or impression that is often difficult to describe or difficult to put into words.

Haven't we all said at times: "I have a feeling s/he likes me", or something like: "I 've got a feeling s/he is lying."

This type of feeling is called intuition or gut feeling. Body language plays a big role in intuition, as it gives us messages about the other person that we can interpret at a sub-conscious level. It is therefore necessary to get to know our own body language first. What little mannerisms do we exhibit if we're lying or find someone attractive? Be aware of them and try and consciously modify them. Write down your mannerisms in your EI Journal.

Every stance, every movement, every gaze is a message sent from within. The eyes communicate more than any other part of the human anatomy. Staring or gazing at others can create pressure and tension in many situations; gangs have fought over the way someone has looked at them and we've all sat next to the unnerving person on the bus who stares or invades our personal space. Researchers suggest that individuals who can out-gaze another person can develop a sense of control and power over others not so inclined – think of Svengali in Daphne du Maurier's book. On the other hand, the eyes can convey feelings of love or attraction, as well as being 'negative'.

Whoever said that the eyes are the windows to the soul was spot on. The eyes are the best non-verbal indicator of our emotional and intellectual state of mind.

We think of those who will not look us in the eye as untrustworthy, dishonest, afraid or insecure. We think of those who have alert, expressive eyes as intelligent, energetic, and emotional. Our eyes have the power to judge, to attract, and to frighten. Through our eyes we can show interest, boredom, disbelief, surprise, terror, disgust, approval, and disapproval. Many parents can bring their children to tears, for example, without saying a word – just by looking at them.

Maintained eye contact can show if a person is trustworthy,

sincere or caring. Shifty eyes, too much blinking or even too still a gaze can suggest deception. People with eye movements that are relaxed and comfortable, yet attentive to the person they are conversing with, are seen as more sincere and honest. The eyebrow muscle draws the eyebrows down and toward the centre of the face if someone is annoyed. If someone is truly empathetic and caring during a conversation the eyebrows will not show the annoyed facial grimace. However, we need to pay attention to the culture or species we are trying to communicate with or we can get it badly wrong. For example, in certain cultures, looking a 'superior' in the eye will not be tolerated and staring at a cat with wide eyes is a show of hostility – handy to know if you ever need to speak cat.

The mouth is also a great communicator and not just for talking – and, yes, kissing can be a great form of communication, before you ask! There are 50 or so different types of human smiles. By analyzing the movements of over 80 facial muscles involved in smiling, researchers can tell when a smile is true and sincere. Look for the crinkle in the skin at the middle, outside corner of the eyes and if it is not there, the smile is probably fake. Authentic smiles are smiles that 'crest' or change rapidly from a small facial movement to a broad open expression.

There is an expression about people whose smile doesn't reach their eyes – we've all known people like that and we have probably all sensed that they're not very nice. Similarly, if someone's mouth is drawn in a thin, tight line then they probably aren't happy – in fact, they're probably furious. What do you think if someone has a 'fixed' grin or smile on their face? Could it be because behind those lips they're gritting their teeth....?

Think of all the people you know well and imagine their faces in repose. There will be people you think of as miserable, whose mouths will be set in the downward curve, while you will see others with a smiley face most times. The little Emoticons you get on computers are just pictorial representations of basic human mouth expression – and think how much emotions those little curves can convey.

Bodily cues are the most reliable of all non-verbal signals of deception because a person generally has less conscious control over these than other signals. Hand-to-face gestures and shrugs are strong markers of deception. Playing with or touching things nearby during conversations has been found to be associated with deception. Deceivers are also likely to use their hands and arms in a quick and animated way during speech. And, no we're not picking on Tony Blair – pick any politician. Many of them go to acting coaches to actually learn how to cover up their natural body language and what physical gestures to learn to convey sincerity.

Ironically, as we have said, silence can also be used to communicate with great effect. More and lengthier pauses during conversation; a lot of sounds such as "uh" "um" and/or word repetitions; less lengthy answers or explanations where they would be expected to be, can all be taken as indicators of deception. While silence when expecting a positive answer can be an indication that the response would be negative if the person felt strong enough to respond verbally. Often silence is the best course of action when you can't decide what to say or if you know that what you say could escalate into a disagreement. Sir William Osler thought so too:

'Look wise, say nothing, and grunt. Speech was given to conceal thought.'

Even the space a person leaves around themselves can be an indicator of personality or mood. Everyone needs their own physical personal space and if it is invaded intentionally or by oversight can cause an individual to feel uncomfortable or threatened.

Studies have shown that those individuals who do not respect space will be less popular and often rejected by others. To measure personal space, extend your arms out in front of you with your fingers pointing away from you. Sweep around yourself 360 degrees and this will indicate your normal personal space area. If we go back to the odd person on the bus or think of the bore at the party, a large part of our discomfort will stem from the fact that they have invaded our space.

Hand signals can communicate without the use of any speech – and many of them are extremely rude! There are universal hand gestures, which communicate certain feelings. However, be careful! These gestures may not be as universal as we would like to think...

It is important to note that the same gestures have different meanings in different cultures and different situations. Making the 'all OK' sign by making a circle with your thumb and forefinger works well under water but means something extremely rude in Latin American countries.

How we can interpret body language depends on the given situation, the culture, the relationship we have with the person as well as the gender of the other person. If you don't take this into account, you may find yourself in hot water with the locals.

Physical movements also communicate. For example, touching can be comforting, scary, friendly or aggressive. The use of touch should be a lesson in a master class of body language, as it can be used very effectively by deceivers. If we think of politicians again, those of us proficient in body language reading are nauseated by watching the posturing that goes on – the double clasp of the hand while looking into the other person's eyes, while all the time we know that the two men hate each other – while other onlookers may be taken in by the whole charade.

Even the way a person stands or walks reflects their level of confidence or comfort level. Generally speaking, the more a person moves around, the less kudos will be given to them. Interestingly, because women are more communicative in general, while men are more analytical, they use both verbal and nonverbal cues more frequently in their communication with others.

A study conducted on the way women and men enter a room illuminates this. On average, women exhibited 27 distinctive body movements when making their entrance while men only displayed 12.

On the surface one might think this difference in initial expressive gestures relates only to the fact that women are more outwardly expressive of their emotions. But there is actually a much more important implication: When observers are asked to rate the estimated power or status of a person entering a room, they give higher ratings to people who make fewer physical gestures. So, girls, keep still if you want respect.

On the subject of posture, it's worth remembering that aggressors usually attack weaker specimens given a choice. Just think how often we have watched wildlife films of a predator stalking the youngest, oldest or generally easiest potential prey. On a survival basis we are animals as much as the lion or cheetah, so in potentially dangerous situations, avoid exhibiting 'prey' signals.

When walking home or waiting at a bus stop on your own, stay upright, walk confidently and keep any movement as slight as possible. Just as a shark will home in on a struggling fish, a potential attacker will home in on the subconscious signs of unease you may be displaying. Sad to say, people exhibiting 'victim' signals will often become just that.

Have you ever had the feeling that you have just been lied to but can't pinpoint how you know it? The words of the conversation probably weren't what made us think this. It was more likely to have been the body movements and signals that gave the other person away. Darting eyes, not showing their palms, shifting from one foot to another, their hand covering their mouth or twiddling their earlobe are all clues. Remember though that these are just clues. Not everyone will necessarily be lying if they do these things. It's just that they have just made your danger radar 'ping' and you would be wise to proceed with caution.

When we pick up on these clues our subconscious, instinct or gut feeling decodes them and tells us that the words and gestures don't match. As we have said before, whenever there is a conflict between the words that someone says and their body signals and movements, we almost always believe their body.

Once you become aware of body language and its importance, you will naturally become more of an observer of people.

Quick exercise – People Watching

Sit in a café or at a bus stop and surreptitiously watch the people around you, particularly those in conversation with others. We say surreptitiously, as otherwise you could get into trouble for paying too much unwelcome attention. The trick is to appear to be the next J K Rowling, writing your great work in a café, while actually you're making notes in your Emotional Journal.

Try and work out what sort of relationship these two people are having. Are they lovers, casual friends, family members, acquaintances, strangers or old friends? What is the tone of their discussion? Is there much bodily movement or more words or vice versa?

It's also interesting to note their nationality, as it is true that southern Europeans, for example, use their hands more than the northern Europeans – this could be an evolutionary response to do with cold and extremities – no doubt someone will let us know.

Pay particular attention to their eye movement, hand gestures, tone of voice and posture and make notes on what you think the conversation is about, who the dominant participant is and what their moods are – which might be different or conflicting.

Doing exercises like this is great fun and very informative. If you're lucky enough to be near enough to overhear their conversation it can be even more fascinating, as you can catch the subconscious lies and almost watch another person's danger radar 'ping' or watch them completely ignoring it. It's much easier watching other people communicate non-verbally than doing it yourself, as when you are communicating, you're focusing on what you want to say and what the other person is saying rather than on your own or their body language.

To help you learn the basic, we have prepared a list of what to look for in various situations, although the nuances and variations are almost endless. However, in any meeting, the following usually apply:

Being receptive

If you want to appear receptive in a meeting of any sort, keep your arms, legs, and feet relaxed and uncrossed. If you are wearing a jacket, open it up. It relays the message... "I am being open and honest with you." Think back to any situation where you 'knew' the other person didn't want to listen. Bet they had their arms folded defensively across their chest. Similarly, if you want to appear receptive, follow the same guidelines. You may be surprised at how much you want to fold your arms if you start hearing things you don't want to hear.

Appearing interested

Taking into account their personal space, move to within six to eight feet of the other person and lean slightly forward, keeping your body as straight as you can. Interested people always pay attention and lean forward. Leaning backwards or turning your body away from the other person demonstrates aloofness or rejection. Consequently, look for that when other people are talking to you. Maintain eye contact as much as you can without staring – it's a fine line.

Mirroring

This means copying, which we probably all did as a child. Pay attention to the other person's breathing and the pace at which they are talking. Is it fast or slow? Without being obvious, mirror them. If they cross their legs, slowly do the same. If they put their head on one side, wait a few seconds then casually copy them. This is a skill, which if learned properly, is a very powerful tool. You can use it to defuse situations, calm anger, build rapport and make people more receptive to you. We come back to mirroring later and have touched on it before. Use it carefully and be aware when it is being done to you, as it can be very manipulative in the hands of practiced deceivers.

Building rapport

Keep good eye contact but try not to stare or look elsewhere all the time. Smile as much as is appropriate – you're obviously not going to smile if you're being told bad news. Touch the other person, if appropriate. Just bear in mind the sort of meeting you're having and the gender, culture and status of the person you are talking to. Bearing in mind that we usually assess a person in the first 10 seconds, pay attention to how you greet them. If you are shaking hands, make it firm but not bone-crushing and certainly not as if you are handing them a wet fish – nothing is so off-putting. Similarly, if the custom is to kiss, make sure you have researched how many kisses and where. With some cultures it's one cheek, some two, some three and some four. In some cultures, men kiss men but women don't kiss men. Observe or do your research first.

Going back to specific groups, the reason for gender differences in expressive tendency can be traced all the way back to infancy. It seems that baby boys are more likely to be put down early, and are less frequently touched than are girls. Girls are taught from their earliest stages of development that public displays of affection are acceptable, while boys are conditioned to keep their emotions and feelings to themselves. ('Boys don't cry'.) That's why women have no problem hugging others in almost any situation, while men often find it difficult to embrace and show empathy under even the most intimate and private circumstances, which is something that many women find very distressing in close relationships.

There is a huge debate about whether it is possible to have really good friends of the opposite gender without sex rearing its ugly head. We won't even enter into that one, as it could be a book all on its own, however, there are many situations where a man and a woman have to be together and just interact as two people, regardless of gender. In a professional situation, for example, in which a man and a woman are forced into close proximity, one of them might create the appropriate distance by omitting an essential part of the normally seductive body language, or by making it incomplete. For example, they may turn part of their bodies away from each other to eliminate the flirting factor, or may avoid too much direct eye contact. However, if you were to observe the same body language in a clearly personal situation, it might suggest that the two were angry (or even disgusted) with one another.

The trick is to always try and keep the situation in context, which you can only do when the thinking brain works in harmony with the emotional brain. What you don't want to do with your observations is to add two and two and make six; follow your instinct though and remember the 'duck theory'. If it walks like a duck and quacks like a duck – it's probably a duck.

Listening, Not Hearing
Communicating outwards is only part of the equation where information and emotions are concerned. A person can go to a lot of trouble offering information, which then goes to waste if it isn't really taken on board. How often have you spent ages crafting a

letter or email which conveys everything you wanted to say, only to find that the recipient has picked up on one sentence in the first paragraph and 'heard' only that one thought? To be effective, communication has to be via a two way street, which has been swept and has no obstacles. Fat chance with emotions, judgments, history and hierarchy all over the place.

However, we can do our best to really listen deeply to what the other person has to say and understand what they mean. *Hearing* only requires ears that work; it is essentially a passive exercise. *Listening*, on the other hand, requires comprehension, minimal distraction and a release from your opinions (being non-judgmental) while the other person is speaking; it is most definitely an active exercise. Think of the difference between hearing music and really listening to it.

Real listening can take many forms. When speaking with (and notice we use the American and European 'with' instead of the more Anglo Saxon 'to') someone who is listening intently, you may feel as if you are the only person in the world. The listener gives you the impression that s/he is completely entranced by your words and thoughts.

The experience of deep listening seems kind, understanding and meaningful. Deep listening evokes a powerful interaction, a stronger relationship and mutual understanding that helps to decrease friction and conflict. Deep listening is really *being* with another. You're in a state of 'being in the now' where your mind is not cluttered with judgments or thoughts of the future. You feel no urgency or impatience, and you let go of beliefs and prejudices you may have about the other person. You 're not analysing, thinking about your responses, what to have for tea or second-guessing, you're simply letting the feelings and sounds affect you.

In relationships, how often do we complain that our partner doesn't listen to us? Even the response 'I hear you' can be dismissive. This implies that the listener has heard your words but either doesn't believe them or doesn't agree with them. Often this is after you have poured your heart out on a particular subject and you feel crushed by their response.

It has been said that as much as 90% of behaviour problems come from children needing adults to listen to them. One study reported that the number one request from suicidal teenagers was for adults to listen to what they had to say.

When we hear of the tragic suicideof a young person there is a often a diary or a chat room entry saying that they had no-one to talk to, so life wasn't worth living. As parents, relatives, close friends or care-givers, we urge you to really listen to what a child says to you, as you could literally save their life.

Silence is very threatening to many people, which is why i-Pods, radios and TVs are so important. However, nothing can beat human interaction and listening, as being listened to is akin to being loved or cared about. If you have ever spent time in hospital, feeling ill and sorry for yourself, you will know how important it is to have visitors or even to be listened to by the staff. Having no-one to listen to you is like being abandoned.

In the development of a child, it is even more vital. Remember how affected we all were when the plight of the Romanian orphans came to light. Pictures of those isolated, neglected tiny children made everyone cry and it was because we instinctively understand what it is like to be unwanted, ignored and unheard.

Clearly then, we all feel better when we feel heard and understood. In order to be understood, we must be listened to. Often, as adults, it is more important to us to feel heard than to actually get what we said we wanted. On the other hand, feeling ignored and misunderstood can be literally painful whether we are six or sixty. Spoilt brats turn into cantankerous old people and often old age tantrums are just noisy signals saying 'Here I am, listen to me, don't ignore me.'

As with other emotional needs, the need to be heard is a survival need, as we are all interdependent and many of our basic needs depend on the co-operation of others. But first we must know and communicate our needs. For example, the only tool a baby has to draw attention to itself is to cry. Before the mother tunes in to her child, she doesn't know whether the cry means that the baby is hungry, in pain or needs changing but the cry in itself prompts her to check all three, so the cry has been effective. If a baby is ignored when it cries, however, it soon learns not to bother – and that will be with that child for the rest of its life.

On a more mundane level, if we are passengers in a car, say, and we feel unsafe, we must communicate our feelings. If the driver ignores us, our lives may literally be threatened. If we are not heard, we cannot communicate our needs. It is understandable, then, that we feel frustrated or worse when we do not feel heard.

By developing our own listening skills, we can demonstrate them to others. They in turn will become better listeners and we will feel heard, understood and respected. It's the opposite of a vicious circle. Remember that listening to either a child or adult helps them feel heard, understood, important, valued, respected and cared about. And remember that the best listeners focus on feelings, not facts. When we are completely 'in the moment' of rapport with another person, we are connected to a deeper intelligence that is often called instinct or intuition. That means using deep listening to hear beyond the spoken words to the 'essence' of the meaning and to the feelings behind them. Sometimes just holding another person and listening to them cry, rant or say nothing can literally be a life saver.

Miscommunication

Often, it is socially unacceptable or inappropriate to say exactly what we are feeling. It might be that we are too afraid of offending others, too afraid of appearing unhappy or unhealthy or too afraid of social disapproval.

Often, instead of expressing our feelings clearly and directly, we express the same emotions indirectly, either through our actions or our body language. Sometimes we lie about our feelings, or deny them, such as when we answer "fine" to the question "how do you feel about that?" When we start to hide our feelings, lie about them, or tell people only what we think they want to hear, we create an unholy can of communication worms and can then spend a lifetime trying to unravel it.

Let's look at some examples of how we corrupt the language of feelings:

Masking Our Real Feelings

There are many ways we do this. Sometimes we just lie about them, for example when someone says she is "fine" though it is obvious that she is irritated, worried, or stressed. Try being honest the next time someone close to you asks how you are, but don't wallow. For example, if your friend asks how you are and you feel a bit anxious about an imminent meeting, for example, then say so; he or she may be able to give you practical advice. Just don't become one of those moaning minnies who replies "You don't want to know!" People will very soon stop asking you how you feel. Another fine line for you to tread.

Inconsistency

Often, our tone of voice or our body language contradicts the words we are saying. None of us can totally hide our true feelings, but many of us do try to disguise our voices to go along with the act. People who are especially superficial even adopt the cosmetic voices found on television in order to conform to societal expectations, and further mask what they truly feel. The opposite is also true. Have you ever heard a friend speak positively in an overly bright tone and yet known that there was an underlying problem?

Politicians, who are adept at deception, often go to great lengths to conform to an image instead of showing who they really are. Then there are the characters in the soaps. Think of Cilla Battersby-Brown in Coronation Street; when she's trying to wheedle something out of Les or Chesney, she adopts a low, syrupy tone. Once she's thwarted however, she soon reverts to good old fishwife tones.

Overuse / Lack of Vocabulary

One of the ways we corrupt language is to over-use a word. Consider the word 'love'. We love apple pie and custard, a glass of wine, HP sauce, and our mothers. Doesn't it seem there should be a different word for the way we feel about our parents as opposed to food? Hate is another word, which is tremendously overused. If someone hates queues, hates fennel, and hates estate agents, how can they express the strength of their feelings about paedophilia? Try using synonyms, such as like, adore, loathe, abhor, detest or dislike instead. Not only will it convey the strength of your feeling about a particular thing or subject but it will increase your vocabulary and you will become less frustrated about how clearly you express your feelings.

Exaggeration

When we exaggerate our feelings we are trying to get attention. People who need to exaggerate have had their feelings neglected for so long, they have resorted to dramatisation to be noticed and cared about. Unfortunately, when they send out false signals, they can alienate people and risk becoming like the boy who cried wolf. Because those around them are so used to their over-dramatisations, they ignore them when the speaker really needs help.

Consider these exclamations, none of which are typically true in a literal sense: "I feel mortified. I feel devastated. I feel crushed. I feel decimated…" If you feel crushed when you lose your car keys, how do explain how you feel when you lose your job?

Minimisation

The opposite of exaggeration, many people minimise their feelings, particularly when they are upset, worried or depressed. They use expressions such as: "I'm fine." "I'll be all right." "I'm OK," "Don't worry about me." "There's nothing wrong."

Such people typically are either too proud, too scared or feel too unworthy to share their feelings. They desperately need to communicate with others, but they won't allow others to get close to them. They effectively push people away by withholding their true feelings.

Chapter Eight

Empathy

Understanding and Relating To Others

'There can be no knowledge without emotion.
We may be aware of a truth,
Yet, until we have felt its force,
It is not ours.
To the cognition of the brain must be added the experience of the soul.'

We've seen this before, right at the start, but it is a very important quote, which bears repeating. What Arnold Bennett is saying almost sums up the concept of emotional intelligence and certainly describes a person who is able to empathise.

The dictionary definition of empathy is *'the ability to imagine oneself in another's place and understand the other's feelings, desires, ideas, and actions.'*

It is from the German *'einfuhling'* and is apparently a mis-translation of Freud. Many people confuse empathy with sympathy but the key differences are that someone feeling empathy can truly understand and imagine the plight of another, while someone feeling sympathy understands that the other person is suffering but has never experienced that plight, nor can s/he imagine what it would be like to suffer it.

Empathy should be innate – neurologists say that empathy starts to develop in a normal person at around two and is completely developed by their late teens – but it can be arrested in its development, depending on the child's development. It is effectively a complex mix of reasoning and emotion.

To show empathy is to identify with another 's feelings. The ability to empathise is directly dependent on your ability to feel your own feelings and identify them. If you have never felt a certain emotion, it will be harder for you to understand how another person is feeling when experiencing it.

If, for example, you have never experienced the death of a loved one, you will not know how intense that pain can be. If you have never been in love, you will not understand its power. Similarly, if you have never felt jealous or bitter, you will not understand those feelings.

Reading about a feeling and intellectually knowing about it is very different from actually experiencing it for yourself. Maybe this is why the best therapists are usually those who have 'been around the block'. On the other hand, when we say that someone can't relate to other people, it is likely because they haven't experienced, acknowledged or accepted many feelings of their own.

Once you have been bullied, for example, it is much easier to relate with someone else who has been bullied. Our innate emotional intelligence gives us the ability to quickly recall those instances and form associations when we encounter bullying again. We then can use the reliving of those emotions to guide our thinking and actions. Often, when someone has been through the emotional mill and come out the other side, they feel motivated to use their experience to not only empathise but to help others who are experiencing the same thing.

In order to feel empathy then, we must first be able to experience our own emotions, which we have already covered. Without self-awareness or emotional literacy, there can be little empathy. Empathy is another cornerstone of emotional intelligence and is a pre-requisite for compassion. People who are good at identifying others ' emotions and persuading others to respond in a desirable manner are demonstrably more successful in their work and social lives.

We can show empathy by acknowledging the emotion. We may say, for example,

'It's perfectly appropriate for you to be angry about that' or *'I can understand why you would be depressed.'*

We can also show empathy through a physical movement such as hug or a touch. Though empathy is usually used in reference to sensing someone else's painful feelings, it can also apply to someone's positive feelings of success, accomplishment, pride or achievement. In this case a literal 'pat on the back' would also be a sign of empathy, as is a hug when you know that the other person is down.

Sensitivity

In one of the Mayer et al studies, many variables were measured. Of these, sensitivity was found to have the highest correlation to emotional intelligence. By definition, sensitive people are more likely to notice someone else's feelings and to feel something themselves. But even those who are not naturally sensitive, or do not have a high natural emotional intelligence level, can take steps to show more sensitivity to the feelings of others.

Sensitivity also means being receptive to others' cues, particularly the non-verbal ones such as facial expressions. This is similar to a highly sensitive radio antenna, which can pick up faint signals. The more information you are able to receive, the more you can help others and yourself.

Compassion

Empathy is closely related to compassion. It seems to both precede compassion and be a prerequisite for it. When we feel empathy for someone we are getting emotional information about them and their situation. By collecting information about other people's feelings, you get to know them better. As you get to know others on an emotional level, you are likely to see similarities between your feelings and theirs, and between your basic emotional needs and theirs.

When you realise that someone else's basic emotional needs are similar to yours, you are more able to identify with them, relate to them and empathise with them. For example, a compassionate mother anywhere in the world would be able to empathise with the suffering of another mother, even in another continent.

All humans have similar emotional needs, as Maslow pointed out. The wide variety among our needs is mostly a difference in degree, rather than in type. For example, we all need to feel some degree of freedom, but I may need more than you, or vice versa.

Compassion can be defined as a combination of empathy and understanding. Greater empathy gives you greater information, and the more information you have on something, the more likely you are to understand it. Higher emotional intelligence makes possible a greater capacity for such understanding. Thus, the logical sequence is as follows: Higher emotional sensitivity and awareness leads to higher levels of empathy. This leads to higher levels of understanding, which then leads to higher levels of compassion.

Conscience

Those who are not in touch with their own feelings are not likely to have a sense of conscience. They may feel no remorse or guilt for causing harm to others because they don't allow their own emotions to become painful to them – it would be too dangerous. Or they may be devoid of empathy, such as those with psychopathic tendencies.

One trigger, which could easily cause a person to lose touch with his own feelings and to lose his natural sense of conscience, is an extremely painful childhood and adolescence. Such people have experienced so much pain that they shut themselves away from it. This pain may have come from physical, sexual or emotional abuse. The end result, though, is similar.

They do not experience their own pain (because they have buried it), so they have no understanding of the pain of another. Therefore, nor do they have any empathy. This is why our study of the Inner Child is so important.

They are also likely to be extremely needy. In other words they may have many, deep, unmet emotional needs. As adults, they will have developed elaborate defence mechanisms in an attempt to block the pain coming from both their unmet emotional needs and from the guilt they would feel if they allowed themselves to feel.

As Freud helped us see, attempts to defend our brains from psychological pain usually involve the cognitive parts of the brain, which, as we have explored, are not strong enough to defend us from powerful emotional responses. What the cognitive brain is very good at, however, is covering up these emotional responses in the guise of rationalisation, justification, denial, intellectualisation, moralising, preaching, self-righteousness, projection, and suppression.

We are sure that you can all think of people who fall into the categories above; they all have huge un-met needs, often from great trauma in childhood, but they mask them under the cloak of being totally in control, denying that they have any problems or telling others how they should live their own lives.

Think about people in the public eye who have been found to have feet of clay. Good examples are religious leaders, who preach one code but practise another. The masks they operate under are preaching, moralising and self-righteousness. Other people who live according to the 'do what I say, not what I do' code could be parents, teachers and politicians. How many of them do you think actually practise what they preach?

In the absence of a conscience, behaviour can only be controlled by fear, threats and punishment or by separation from society. This comes at tremendous social (and physical)[1] cost, and evidently is ineffective, given prisons at bursting point, designer tagging being fashionable, community punishments and rising fines.

But could we argue that laws are really only needed when individual conscience has failed? If the individual has no framework – and we will explore that in more depth later – then society (aka government) must impose one in order for society to function.

Unfortunately, in many countries, the thinking behind the framework itself is damaged, because of the generally low value each government places on feelings and emotions. Until very recently few people in authority seem to have appreciated or even ever thought of the evolutionary value of our feelings and emotions.

Thankfully that is now changing, albeit slowly. In the UK, for example, starting to give lessons in EQ to schools could be the beginning of a new moral code or framework for a new generation. But we are back to the pendulum effect.

In our schooldays we didn't learn about emotions or how to be 'touchy-feely' – a terrible put down – but we were given a very strong moral framework within which to work and we were taught respect for – if not fear of – authority. In the last 30 years the pendulum swung to an 'anything goes' attitude, probably inculcated by the same people who had been cowed by the previous way of thinking.

Unfortunately, no government seems to have realised that neither method can work without aspects of the other. We're back to balance.

Emotions need to be explored, acknowledged and labelled but not at the expense of respect and empathy. Too much rigidity and denial of emotions causes us to place more importance on 'looking after number one', which creates a 'me first' society, even at the expense of our own children. There is a fine line between selfishness and lack of responsibility. Think of the shocking cases recently involving mothers who left their children at home while they went out enjoying themselves or even on holiday. These women were putting their needs and desires above those of their children, even though the children were too young to take care of themselves.

This is a worrying trend for the future and is borne out by a report from June 2007, which says that 'studies carried out by leading children's charity NCH found a 100% increase in the prevalence of emotional problems and conduct disorders among young people since the 1930s'.

The charity defines an 'emotionally well' child as *one who demonstrates empathy, self-awareness, an ability to manage their feelings, motivation and good social skills* – all the basic tenets of emotional intelligence. A child with parents who demonstrate irresponsible behaviour, lack of care and extreme selfishness is unlikely to grow up well-adjusted.

Morality/Ethics

'It is really the mistake of our age. We think it is enough to discover new things, but we don't realise that knowing more demands a corresponding development of morality.'
Jung

It might seem odd to discuss morality and ethics in a book on Emotional Intelligence but Jung sums it up in this quote. We again come across the supposed polarity between thinking and feeling. Also, we have drawn heavily on Daniel Goleman's writings on Emotional Intelligence and he says quite a lot about morality and ethics in his 1995 work. His chapter on empathy has a sub-heading:

'Empathy and Ethics: The Roots of Altruism'.

In this section he talks of the link between empathy and caring, saying that, to the empathetic (ie. emotionally intelligent) person, another person's pain is also their own and that the 'empathetic attitude is engaged again and again in moral judgments'.

He uses various examples; ones we could use are:

- Should you tell your best friend if you know their husband/wife is having an affair?
- Should you take paperclips home from work?
- Should you take sides in a war?
- Should you give money to charity?
- Should you intervene in a domestic argument?
- Should you take cash you find in the street to a police station?

He goes on to say that a virtuous life, as most philosophers have observed, is based on self-control.

In his millennial essay 'Sorry, but Your Soul Just Died' Tom Wolfe worried that when science has killed the soul, *'the lurid carnival that will ensue may make the phrase "the total eclipse of all values" seem tame.'*

This brings us back to polarity and one swing of the pendulum or the other. Wolfe's quote pre-supposes that humanity will totally embrace science (rationality), which will kill feeling.

In our context it means that we will ignore emotions and stick with cognitive reasoning; the truth, of course, is that a being as evolved as a human *cannot* suppress his or her emotional aspects.

We would go further and say, as Maslow does, that there is another tier beyond rationality and emotions and that is spirituality. Whether a person is religious in a formal sense or not, most people agree that there is a spiritual side to life and it is usually (although by no means always) this element in a person's make up which determines their morality or code of ethics.

If we agree with Goleman that the roots of morality are found in empathy, then empathic affect or putting oneself in another's place must lead us to follow certain moral principles. But where do these moral principles come from? Are they innate or are they observed in parents, peers and the external world?

In the last chapter we discussed the depression in children and young people and it seems to us that this often stems from having no moral or value compass. It may also be that children who have never experienced values in those who should show them the way forward, will grow up to pass this vacuum on to their own children. It would appear that, if children are to learn society's rules, they need to absorb and integrate a rudimentary understanding of kindness and caring from watching adult models.

According to research, the opportunities most likely to enhance the development of empathy and morality in adolescents are:

- A parent committed to a cause
- Service opportunities during adolescence
- Cross-cultural experiences
- A rich mentoring experience in young adulthood.

If these opportunities can be offered to adolescents, they will generally grow into adults who will demonstrate in their lives a lifelong, passionate commitment to their life pursuits and they will develop appropriate trust, courage, and responsible imagination. However, if these opportunities are not on offer, then we are heading for a moral abyss.

One of the most important things parents or care-givers (teachers, social services, foster parents, step parents) can do for their young children and adolescents is to demonstrate moral behaviour rather than preach about it – do as I do, not do as I say.

It is important for a child to learn empathy, but that child must also learn what to do with that empathy. It is also important to avoid being judgemental, as we mention right at the start of the book.

Understanding that we are all made up of the same emotions and intelligence but may have had vastly different experiences in life can help in treating others with fairness. Another good phrase to remember is *'there but for the grace of God go I'*.

Chapter Nine

Management & Motivation

Using Your Emotional Intelligence

Emotional management can be used internally or externally. When we manage our own emotions we are able to understand and take responsibility for them. We realise that we are in control of our own destiny, even if our current situation means that we are free only in the way that we think and feel. On an internal basis, managing our own emotions means that we can separate healthy from unhealthy feelings and can change our moods from negative to positive. It means that we can realise that any experience can be turned into a positive learning and growing opportunity.

Like any steps, it is better for us if we take them one at a time and in the correct order. Get to grips with yourself before you try and help others or point out their emotions to them. It is crucial for us to understand and accept ourselves before we can help anyone else. Anything else is out of balance.

Optimism

Motivation, hope and optimism are often intertwined. A basic question to ask anyone is 'What makes you do so and so on a regular basis?' This could be anything from getting up in the morning to training for a marathon. If the person doing either activity had no hope in a future – even if that future is only tomorrow – then what would be the point? If they have hope, then they can have optimism, as tomorrow may be better than today. Without hope there can be no optimism.

Martin Seligman, who conducts research on positive psychology in America, has developed the concept of 'learned optimism' which means optimism as a learned response rather than an innate one. In his research, Seligman found that when faced with setbacks, optimists tend to make specific, temporary, causal attributions to factors outside themselves, while pessimists make global, permanent and internal attributions. It's a bit like the difference between Pooh Bear and Eeyore. Pooh is a natural optimist who could never believe that the grey cloud is there to rain specifically on him. Eeyore, on the other hand. is sure that life is out to get him personally.

On a more prosaic basis, Seligman's research showed that salesmen who were optimists sold 37% more insurance in their first two years than pessimists.

It's a 'triumph of optimism over experience', as Oscar Wilde would say. We might say that it's the ability to bounce back from adversity. The ability to manage our feelings and handle stress is another aspect of Emotional Intelligence that ensures success.

Optimists are generally understood to be born not made and yet it is possible to learn optimism. We are back to how we view any situation.

There is a beautiful Japanese haiku, which says:

'My barn having burned to the ground, I can now see the moon.'

You might call it being a Pollyanna, but it really is possible to see something positive in any situation and to hope for something better. A good question to ask yourself if faced with a catastrophe is: 'What are my alternatives?' or 'What will achieve more – weeping and wailing and blaming everyone else? or looking on the bright side, however faint and far away that brightness may be?'

In making this point that an optimistic response can be learned, we are in no way trying to belittle depression. Clinical depression is a crippling problem invoking great pain in the sufferer. They are almost literally bereft of hope, without which there is no possibility of optimism. However, when a person has given up on hope, they have given up on themselves. What they haven't realised is that their only hope *is* themselves, that we cannot rely on anyone else for our happiness.

We may think that our happiness is in the hands of our parents, our partner, our children or some other person, but it isn't. Of course, all these people contribute to our wellbeing or lack of it, but ultimately, we live mostly with ourselves and if you are not happy with yourself then you can't truly be happy with anyone else.

'I never loved another person the way I loved myself.'
Mae West

Why do you think it is called self-motivation? Might it be because it comes from yourself? Self-motivation is the ability to use your emotions to cause yourself to take positive action, whatever that means to you; to continue to persistently pursue your goals even in the face of adversity or obstacles. It is about using your emotions to be enthusiastic, optimistic, confident, and persistent rather than lethargic, pessimistic and constantly second-guessing yourself and your decisions.

Purpose

What is life without purpose and goals? You have used your SWOON chart to consider what makes you happy and motivated in life.

First, identify your basic needs and whether you have met them, then consider what the icing is on your cake of life.

Even in these uncertain, ginancially unstable times the average standard of living is better now than at any time in history. Take any measure you like – home ownership, car ownership, earnings, spending power, advances in medicine, the holidays we take. We have never had it so good. Surely this is the golden age of opportunity and the good things in life.

But are you really any happier than your grandparents or parents were at your age? The answer is probably not. In fact, statistically, you are more likely to be unhappy or even miserable.

Research shows that ten times more people suffer from major depression now than 60 years ago, with the greatest increase in depression seen in the young, right through from primary school age anxiety, teenage angst, to people in their prime in their thirties. The NCH study bears this out. People are less satisfied and less happy than at any time in recent history.

Think of how much fanfare there was with the advent of the National Lottery and the amounts of money people spend on it. But, believe it or not, a year after their win, research has shown that more than half of the big lottery winners are no happier than before their big cash windfall. They expected money to be the answer to all their problems and the solution to happiness and fulfilment. After the short-term buzz, they were left still looking for the key to real happiness: something money can't buy. So why is this?

People with money acquire lots of material stuff, but when that doesn't make them happy they assume that they need more or different stuff – high definition televisions, this season's fashion, exotic foreign holidays, watches that tell the time on the moon. But the truth is, no amount of 'stuff' will ever be enough unless they can be happy in their own company. Remember that our doctor and barrister are wealthy men. Of course, we're not decrying money – everyone has to eat and have a roof over their head and, given the choice, most of us would prefer a few extra quid in our pockets. As the wonderful Mae West pointed out, *'I've been rich and I've been poor and believe me, rich is better!'* But the really influential factors in the happiness mix are stable relationships, a sound acceptance of oneself, and good health – and the big secret is having a goal or a purpose in life.

Perseverance

What your purpose is in life is a very individual thing and only you can decide what it is. Use your SWOON chart to help you in this. However, the unifying trait when trying to achieve anything is being sufficiently motivated to practise or persevere until you reach your goal.

As Einstein once modestly said:

'It's not that I'm so smart, it's just that I stay with problems longer.'

JK Rowling had the Harry Potter books rejected by 12 publishers before it was snapped up by Bloomsbury; she had written the first one out by hand and on an old manual typewriter, as she couldn't afford a word processor. The key is, she persevered and she always hoped that the next letter would be an offer, which eventually it was.

Madonna reinvents herself every few years because nothing static ever truly succeeds. There are any number of quotes and examples we could use here to illustrate the power of perseverance but you can use your own. Just make sure that you practise it.

Building Trust and Rapport

Rapport is defined as having sympathy, empathy, understanding and an emotional bond with someone else. Trust and rapport are hugely important in managing relationships. People high in emotional intelligence are naturally good at managing trusting relationships. However, to trust and be trusted are skills that can be learned, although it may take some time.

Have you ever had the experience of meeting someone you just click with, where, even if you are seeing them for the first time, this person feels like an old friend? This is what psychologists call instant rapport. Being able to get into rapport with other people is not just a key for successful influence, it is also one of the most fun, enjoyable and relaxing skills you can learn. People like to be around people who can get into rapport with them. People like people who like them and they certainly buy from them, so if you are in sales, pay particular note.

Researchers have noticed that people talking to each other begin unconsciously to co-ordinate their movements, including finger movements, eye blinks and head nods. When they were monitored using electroencephalographs, it was found that some of their brain waves were spiking at the same moment too. As the conversations progressed, these people were getting into rapport with each other. People who say that they can see auras (energy fields) around people and things report flashes of different colours and spikes of energy between people in conversation.

The phenomenon of rapport is well known in the world of therapy and neuro-linguistic programming (NLP) as a starting-point for influential communication. It is mentioned in countless hypnotherapy, NLP and self-help books and is included in most sales training programmes. Yet what is rapport, and how can you use it to help yourself and others?

Rapport has been described as what happens when we get the attention of someone's unconscious mind, and meet them at their 'map of their world'. It is more commonly understood as the sense of ease and connection that develops when you are interacting with someone you trust and feel comfortable with. Rapport emerges when people are in-sync with each other.

Rapport is usually mutual. On a basic level, we usually like people who are like us, so it makes sense that one way to help rapport to develop is to mirror aspects of those we wish to influence. As we discussed in the body language section, any observable behaviour can be mirrored, however, a few notes of caution are appropriate:

- Mirroring is not the same as mimicry. It should be subtle and respectful.

- Mirroring can lead to you sharing the other person's experience. Avoid mirroring people who are in distress or who have severe mental issues.

- Mirroring can build a deep sense of trust quickly. You then have a responsibility to use that trust ethically.

We've all read the articles in magazines and books on how to make people like you or how to find and keep a partner. The key is to be *genuine* in your intentions. Think of the descriptions given to people who have these skills but are not genuine or who do not use their trust ethically – con men, smoothies, charmers, manipulators and even psychopaths.

Building rapport is important in teamwork, leadership and management. Each time we communicate with someone it is usually with a desired outcome in mind. These aims can be simple or complex. Being able to communicate effectively is a skill in its own right. It can be an effective tool in business, management and social policy as long as you have in mind what you want to achieve from the interaction.

There are many ways to manage and motivate others and it depends on the situation and the relationship you have with the other person. You will find a number of exercises to help you with this in the section on Building Rapport.

Chapter Ten

The Application of Emotional Intelligence

Let's Do It!

We were having a discussion the other day about numeracy and we agreed that it was all very well understanding how to add up, subtract and multiply but if the person didn't learn how to apply that knowledge then the knowledge in itself is useless. It's exactly the same with Emotional Intelligence. Hopefully you are reading this book to bring about change in your life and will apply what you have read in a practical way.

Living An Authentic, Emotionally Intelligent Life

'My great mistake, the fault for which I can't forgive myself, is that one day I ceased my obstinate pursuit of my own individuality.'
Oscar Wilde

You may think that between them, Oscar Wilde, Jung and Arnold Bennett have written this book. Indeed, if one looks at any great thinker, writer or leader from any point in history, one can find perfect quotations on how to live an emotionally intelligent life – it's just that that wasn't what it was called then. Back in 1928, for example, Arnold Bennett wrote a wonderful, very short book called How To Live On 24 Hours A Day. It was probably one of the first, non-religious self-help books of its time. In Chapter 8 he talks about living an authentic life in the pursuit of happiness. To paraphrase this part of the book, he says that a person's values or principles should be their guidebook as to how they live their life and that the way they behave can only be in accord with their values by means of ' *daily examination, reflection and resolution'*. He goes on to say that only by living in this way can a person be happy and that we should live more by our instincts than by our reasoning.

Where Bennett uses principles, we often use values or beliefs and by now, through the SWOON exercise, you should have a list of what your values are. You have discovered what turns you off and turns you on. Now what?

Do you remember the dreams you used to have as a child? All children, except those in horrifically abusive relationships, fantasise about their future. Children live by feeling rather than thinking and so are much more in tune with their inner being. Childhood is where hope and optimism are forged or squashed. If you are lucky enough to have had a reasonably happy childhood, remember who you were and where you wanted to go or what you wanted to be before life came and bit you on the backside. Remember the values and beliefs you used to have when you were a young adult, which have been buried under the mental and emotional baggage you have accumulated over all these years. Don't let your experiences of life anchor you in a rut. Polish off those dreams and ambitions and hold them up again as a compass to your future, whatever your age or situation.

There is a lovely saying by Satchel Paige, which we keep pinned to our fridge, which says:

'Work like you don't need the money, love like you've never been hurt, and dance like no one is watching.'

Get back in touch with yourself by meditating, keeping a journal of your hopes and dreams, – your EI journal would be perfect - going for walks on your own, starting to read again. Whatever methods you use to get back in touch with yourself, make them a habit (21 times, remember) and just wait for the ideas and the values to come flooding back.

You have to let your emotions work with your thinking. Remember what Bennett said about reflection. Turn off the TV and find out about yourself, then dare to dream those dreams you used to have. Find out for yourself what is inside you and stop being scared.

'Twenty years from now you will be more disappointed by the things you didn't do than by the ones you did do. So throw off the bowlines. Sail away from the safe harbor. Catch the trade winds in your sails. Explore. Dream. Discover.'
Mark Twain

You are you all the time but in continuous change, so go with the flow. Just love every minute of every day and go where it takes you. Whatever you're doing, just be in that moment, even if it is something as everyday as cleaning your teeth.

Tune into being responsible for yourself. Every decision to do with you is yours and yours alone. Let go of the fears, ignore the cries of 'selfish' and be free. Let go of the 'I must do this for X' or 'I couldn't do that, what would Y think?' Stop thinking *'I can't do that'* or *'I'm too scared.'* You can do anything you want and you can be braver than you think. Being responsible for yourself means realising it's all up to you. It's your life, your decisions, and your choices. There is always a choice and you should take it positively. And if you make the 'wrong' one, learn from it and move on. Two of the saddest words in the English language are 'if only.....'

Being Free To Live Your Life

Viktor Frankl (1905 – 1997) was an Austrian neurologist and psychiatrist who survived the concentration camps and drew a lot of his writing and research from the horrific time he spent there. While this is an extreme example for those of us in the modern West, he sums up the importance of freedom of choice in the emotionally intelligent when he says:

'Everything can be taken from a man but one thing: the last of the human freedoms - to choose one's attitude in any given set of circumstances, to choose one's own way.'

Freedom is the state of accepting who you are, and being responsible for your own decisions. But that simple statement is very profound. Every time you say *'I can't'* find out who that critical voice in your head belongs to. Every time you turn away from what you really want, find out who or what is making you do that. If it is an identifiable voice – your mother's, your old teacher's, then ask what business they have being in *your* head making *your* decisions. It's your choice so you decide.

Enjoy the freedom of choice and be free. Each positive decision begets another one, and another one. Being free means that you always look for the choice (and there always is at least one in any situation), and then make it positively and stick by it.

You may be reading this and thinking, 'It's all right for them to talk, *they* don't have this or that happening to them or haven't lost what I have'. We see it in our workshops all the time. Being at rock bottom is a grim place to be. We know that; we've been there and we're not belittling it, nor are we saying that you can wave a magic wand and make it all OK – you can't. If you are currently in a bad place, you will have to go through your own dark night of the soul and you can't take anyone else with you. There will be people cheering you on from the sidelines but they can't feel your feelings for you, even if they desperately wish they could.

As we have said earlier, start with baby steps and accept that you cannot go from the depths to the heights in any sustained way in a single bound. Just live each day and congratulate yourself for all your achievements, cry if you need to and don't beat yourself up when you don't do as well as you think you might have. For every two steps forward you will have to take one back but you will still have made progress.

You might start with your physical self, as our physical being has effects and consequences on our other beings. If we are physically tired or if we ignore ourselves physically it can have a direct effect on our emotions. Posture is a good example. If we stand tall, shoulders back and smile at the world, we can generally see with a different perspective to that of if we are slumping and frowning. Make your posture tall and wide and open with a greeting smile. You will see the benefits straight away in those you meet or interact with.

If you feel yourself becoming tense or anxious, focus on your breathing – the pattern, the depth, the rhythm. Breathe deeply and evenly for a count of four in and four out. Concentrate and focus and in so doing you distract your conscious mind and become calmer.

Learn to look after yourself. After all, as we have been saying, you are the most important person in your life. Treat yourself as if you were your best friend. Are you tired after a long day? Run yourself a scented bath, light the bathroom with candles and lie back and enjoy the soak.

Some people allow themselves no time at all just to be – they become human doings, not human beings; or they always put others before them and completely ignore themselves. If they live alone they are so afraid of their own company that they clutter their calendar with activity leaving no time for reflection, or they won't cook for themselves and yet would slave away on a meal for others.

Quick exercise – Treating your Best Friend
Make a list in your EI Journal of all the things you would like (and be happy) to do for your best friend, who might be your partner, or a friend. Now ask yourself, 'Would I do that for me?' If not, ask yourself why not. Write down why not underneath each of the

things you have listed.

Once you have self-justified, huffed, puffed and postured you will eventually admit that it is because, unlike the girls in the L'Oréal advert, you actually don't think you're worth it.

From the list, choose one thing you would like someone to do for you and set aside time in your diary to do it for yourself. It might be to buy yourself flowers or perfume or cook yourself a meal. Whatever it is, do it and do it with love, for yourself, then enjoy being loved.

Using our new self we can communicate better with ourselves and better influence and handle other people 's emotions and emotional states. Being able to deal with ourselves and others through emotional awareness influences our lives and destiny. It is a key skill that we should all aspire to in order to maintain and develop relationships, which we have agreed are vital to our happiness.

Try always to acknowledge, accept and understand that other people have their own emotions too. If we accept and acknowledge ourselves and that we are able to control our emotions and can recognise them, then we are better placed to having empathy with others. Always try to bear in mind that everyone has a life and that they, as we, are striving to do the best they can within it.

When dealing with difficult people or situations try transposing yourself in to that other situation. Look at the difficulty from the other person's perspective. Look at how the information takes on a different meaning or has a different emphasis through their eyes. Only then will you be able to better understand what is going on and effectively help to deal with it.

Know yourself, set yourself achievable goals for what you want and need out of life, communicate those wants and needs effectively to yourself and others, change what you need to, to achieve those goals and you will be living an authentic life. Does that sound simple? It can be eventually and you have already taken the first major steps to achieving it.

Well done to you!

Chapter 11

Emotional Intelligence Self-Assessment Questions

Are you emotionally intelligent?

Place each answer in the appropriate answer box, answers chosen should be the closest to your own emotional responses then go to the appropriate page to interpret your score.

1. Your child, against your warnings, runs into a busy road. You pull him/her back to the pavement and:
a] Scold, shout, smack or shake him/her?
b] Master your emotions and calm yourself and explain why it is not a good idea to run in to the road?
c] Master your emotions and decide upon a subsequent punishment?

☐ *Answer*

2. You then:
a] Tell the child off and threaten him/her with dire punishment?
b] Apologise and explain that mum/dad was frightened for their safety?
c] Burst into tears?

☐ *Answer*

3. It annoys you to:
a] Have to make the most of your physical attributes at work?
b] See others making the most of their physical attributes at work?

c] See others unkempt or scruffily dressed at work?

 Answer

4. You are infuriated with your partner. Do you:
a] Refuse to speak for days?
b] Swear and go for a walk?
c] Plot revenge at some future stage?

 Answer

5. Your parent/in-law, is nagging, sarcastic and interfering. Your main feeling is:
a] Resentment?
b] Resignation?
c] Pity?

 Answer

6. Grief is:
a] A necessary and salutary process?
b] Something that time will heal?
c] A blight on your life?

 Answer

7. Does worry serve a purpose?
a] Sometimes?
b] Never?
c] Always?

 Answer

8. You are outraged by a newspaper article/story. Do you:

a] Rant at your friends/family members?
b] Write a letter to the newspaper?
c] Become depressed?

 Answer

9. Is your anger:
a] A spur to change?
b] A spur to hurt or destroy things?
c] Destructive of yourself?

 Answer

10 Time is above all:
a] The greater healer?
b] The great destroyer?
c] To be ignored or defeated and removed?

 Answer

11. A violent crime is:
a] A reflection of a general trend in society today?
b] An isolated, tragic case from which we can draw lessons and from which to learn?
c] An outrage about which something should be done?

 Answer

12. You like music to be
a] Soothing
b] Exciting
c] Deeply moving

 Answer

How well do you know – and like – yourself?

Place each answer in the appropriate answer box, answers chosen should be the closest to your own emotional responses then go to the appropriate page to interpret your score.

Look at the following numbers. How do they appear to you? What impression do you get? How do you immediately define them?

1. 1 – the number one:
a] Solitary?
b] Erect and proud?
c] Slim, tight?

☐ *Answer*

2. 8 – the number eight:
a] Plump, jolly?
b] Fat, squat?
c] Dual, divided?

☐ *Answer*

3. 7 the number seven:
a] Elegant, relaxed?
b] Magical, mystical?
c] Slimy, sidling?

☐ *Answer*

4. Children are most likely to succeed if they read:
a] Fairy tales?
b] Educational books?
c] Historical books?

Answer

5. Nudism is:
a] Beautiful, funny?
b] Disgusting, pathetic?
c] It depends on the bodies?

 Answer

6. How would you describe your body?
a] Unsatisfactory, ugly?
b] Far from perfect but it does its job and attracts other people, which is what matters?
c] Pretty good thank you?

☐ *Answer*

7. You see a very good-looking member of your own sex. Do you feel?
a] Admiration?
b] Envy?
c] Scorn?

☐ *Answer*

8. You have a given name, but always have the choice to use another. If you have not done so, how do you feel about that name?
a] I don't like it. I hate it.
b] I like it. It suits me.
c] It doesn't really suit me but I can't be bothered to change.

☐ *Answer*

9. Involuntary bodily functions inspire:
a] Admiration, wonder?
b] Indifference?
c] Revulsion?

☐ *Answer*

10. Your hero/heroine is/was:
a] A feisty fighter?
b] A victim who fought back?
c] First and foremost a giver, and a star?

☐ *Answer*

11. Life is:
a] A bitch?
b] A party?
c] A battle to be enjoyed?

☐ *Answer*

12. War is:
a] A sorry, inevitable consequence of our beloved human nature?
b] A terrible crime?
c] When we are truly alive and acting to our naturalness?

☐ *Answer*

How Much Self-Confidence Do You Have?

Place each answer in the appropriate answer box, answers chosen should be the closest to your own emotional responses then go to the appropriate page to interpret your score.

1. You are in a foreign country where you have a smattering of the language and cultural knowledge. You want to buy an avocado, a lamb chop and a bottle of wine. Do you:

a] Look up the right words in a dictionary and phrase book?

b] Ask for the goods in your own mother tongue and assume someone will be found who can help you speak or communicate in the foreign language?

c] Have a go at the host country's language coupled with mime and farmyard noises?

☐ *Answer*

2. You hear mocking laughter from a corner as you walk across a room. You:

a] Scowl defiantly?

b] Inspect your clothing and rush for cover?

c] Draw yourself to your full height and smile broadly at the people laughing?

☐ *Answer*

3. Which most closely describes your mood early in the morning?

a] Tetchy and impatient?

b] Jolly and encouraging?

c] Tranquil and purposeful?

☐ *Answer*

4. When you order clothes to be made for you, you order them:

a] Smaller than your current size because you intend to lose some weight?

b] In your current size?

c] With plenty of room for growth?

☐ *Answer*

5. Would a partner's infidelity:
a] Make you feel inadequate?
b] Sadly show up his/her inadequacies?
c] Sadly demonstrate that your relationship is inadequate?

☐ *Answer*

6. You are about to enter by yourself a crowded room full of chattering people. How do you approach it?
a] Resolve to sneak in and skulk in to the corner until you see a familiar face?
b] Assure yourself that you are as bright and attractive as anyone else in the room?
c] Absolutely no problem. A couple of drinks and you will take the party by storm!

☐ *Answer*

7. A person who knows you well ignores your greeting and passes you by without a word or a smile. Do you:
a]   Assume that he/she was preoccupied?
b]   Take offence and brood and worry about it?
c]   Pursue them and ask him/her what was wrong and have you done something wrong?

☐ *Answer*

8. The couple from the apartment above yours have sex noisily during the night. Do you:
a] Feel resentful and bang on the ceiling?

b] Bury your head under your pillow?

c] Wake your partner and whisper that you might as well make similar noises?

 Answer

9. Christmas is:

a] Hell on earth?

b] A magical time?

c] Tough and expensive – but worth it?

 Answer

10. New Year is:

a] Hell on earth?

b] An excuse for a wild party?

c] An excuse for a quiet night in?

[ ] *Answerr*

11. The intolerable thing in a relationship is:

a] Indifference?

b] Infidelity?

c] Arguments?

[ ] *Answer*

12. Your boss holds a door open for you. You:

a] Walk through with a grateful smile

b] Say 'no, please, after you'

c] Walk through saying 'thank you very much'.

[ ] *Answer*

Do You Know What Your Values Are?

Place each answer in the appropriate answer box, answers chosen should be the closest to your own emotional response then go to the appropriate page to interpret your score.

1. Friends and people you respect assure you that a certain sort of music is wonderful. You hear it once and dislike it. Do you:

   a] Pretend to like it?

   b] Openly state your dislike?

   c] Keep an open mind and listen to it again on another occasion?

   □ *Answer*

2. Your best friend's husband/wife is flaunting an affair with a younger partner. Other friends find this amusing. Do you:

   a] Advise the offending party to at least be discreet?

   b] Tell your best friend?

   c] Join in with the secret laughter?

   □ *Answer*

3. Sex for you is?

   a] A way of asserting yourself and gaining pleasure?

   b] A way of surrendering yourself and giving pleasure?

   c] A way of attaining all of these?

   □ *Answer*

4. A crowd roars its approval of a speech. Do you:

   a] Automatically distrust the crowd impulse?

   b] Get caught up in the crowd's approval?

   c] Buy the text and go home and consider?

Answer

5. How often do you leave the phone off the hook or the cell phone switched off?
a] Often – on holidays, in restaurants, in the bath
b] Never – it could be important?
c] Seldom – you like to keep in touch and be available?

 Answer

6. In a restaurant you are served with food that is cold, over-salted or just bad. Do you:
a] Summon the waiter and quietly ask to have the food replaced?
b] Say nothing for fear of an argument or scene?
c] Say nothing until the end of the meal then insist on a reduction on the bill?

 Answer

7. Solitude for a full day or evening is?
a] Intolerable without the radio/television/telephone
b] A delight, a chance to think and recharge the batteries
c] Intolerable, inducing a sense of failure or decline

 Answer

8. Your partner is invited on a company trip abroad. You are:
a] Delighted for them and look forward to seeing some of your own friends
b] Resentful and you will go down to the travel agents on your own account
c] Outwardly supportive but storing recriminations for future use

Answer

9. 'Worry is a horse you whip'... You tend to worry:
a] Never
b] Only when it can lead to a solution
c] All the time

 Answer

10. You are hard pressed for money. A bill arrives in the mail. Do you:
a] Leave it unopened until you can pay it
b] Open it and fall in to depression
c] Open it and instantly telephone the sender to propose terms for settlement

 Answer

11. A lover is:
a] A necessity
b] A luxury
c] A part of the furniture in your life

 Answer

12. Music is:
a] To be heard while doing other things
b] To be listened to while alone
c] To create an atmosphere when with others

 Answer

Is Your Relationship in Danger of Flooding?

We have made constant reference to Daniel Goleman. In Emotional Intelligence he derives the term 'flooding' from another psychologist, John Gottman, to describe the sort of relationship in which aggressive and defensive reflexes have become a way of life between two people. Associations with past hurts, slights, insults, indignities, blind the 'flooded' person to their partner's virtues and strengths and deafens them to the voices of reason. Offence is taken by the most inoffensive remarks; a careless glance is taken as a sneer; natural habits, which had once been seemingly acceptable, even loveable, become irritating beyond endurance. Sometimes, flooding has an identifiable trigger – an infidelity, perhaps, which one party has forgiven in theory but cannot forgive in practice – alcoholism or deceit. Arguments in any relationship are inevitable, some would say are even healthy. What do you think?

Place each answer in the appropriate answer box, answers chosen should be the closest to your own emotional responses then go to the appropriate page to interpret your score.

1. Your partner is:
a] Always difficult and demanding
b] Almost never difficult and demanding
c] Impossible, but okay really

☐ *Answer*

2. You are:
a] Forgiving, tolerant, understanding
b] Passionate, devoted, courteous
c] Impossible, but you love him/her

☐ *Answer*

3. What does the future hold for the two of you?

a] Tough times, but a lot of fun together

b] Tough times, and you have no faith that things will change

c] Roses all the way

 Answer

4. You have financial worries. Your partner caresses you on the sofa. You think:

a] 'Why does s/he always choose the wrong moment?'

b] 'That's a good idea. Let's take time out from those worrisome things.'

c] 'I owe it to him/her to snap out of it and be supportive and resolute.'

 Answer

5. Your partner admires a member of the opposite sex in the street. You feel:

a] Amused

b] Furious

c] 'Here we go again…'

 Answer

6. S/he says 'Darling, we have to talk…' You think:

a] 'Not more of his/her wheedling or browbeating.'

b] 'Oh, Oh…what's gone wrong now?'

c] 'Just what I was going to say.'

 Answer

7. S/he proposes a quite outrageous sexual experiment of a formerly shared fantasy. You:

a] React violently, claiming that you only went along with the fantasy at their request.

b] Ask for time to consider and hope that it will be dropped or forgotten.

c] Think that this may be a little fun.

☐ *Answer*

8. He/she raises an objection to your plans. You say:

a] 'Oh well, forget I ever mentioned it then.'

b] 'Typical. You can't accept any idea which is not your own.'

c] 'Hang on a second darling. Let me think about this.'

☐ *Answer*

9. He/she is always:

a] Enigmatic, confusing, lovely

b] Self-centred, self-absorbed

c] Variable, surprising

☐ *Answer*

10. Loneliness is:

a] Impossible. You always have your own company.

b] A daily experience.

c] Being without your partner.

☐ *Answer*

11. S/he has:

a] Always let you down.

b] Never let you down.

c] Always amused you, so what the hell!

☐ *Answer*

12. He/she is untidy / lazy / inconsiderate to you:
a] As a general rule, yes.
b] Occasionally
c] Never

☐ *Answer*

Visualisations

Visualisation can be a very powerful tool; it can even be a bit scary if you haven't done any before. Just be aware that any emotions, which may well up are coming to the fore for a reason and, if you have allowed them to surface, then you are able to cope with them. Just go with the flow and have some hankies to hand.

If you're doing this on your own, it might be a good idea to record the next bit until you know the routine by heart. Otherwise, ask a friend to read it out to you; it can be a bit disconcerting to have to keep stopping and reading. Do whatever suits you and your situation.

A good time for visualisations is in the morning before you get up. If you are one of those people who doesn't wake until the alarm, then try doing them before you go to sleep at night. They only take around 15 minutes, so you should be able to find some time during the day. Whatever timeyou do them, just give them your full attention.

Always start a visualisation by being in as quiet a space as you can find, preferably where you won't be disturbed. Close your eyes and begin to breathe deeply from your diaphragm, filling your lungs with air. Breathe in for a count of four, then out for a count of four. Once you have done that a few times increase the count to six and then to eight. You will find yourself gradually relaxing and feeling calmer.

If stray thoughts try to interfere with your concentration on your breathing, just push them gently aside and continue to breathe. Some people visualise easier than others but it's a knack anyone can learn. You will soon find what works for you.

For all these visualisations you are going to take yourself to your own, safe, happy place, which only the people and thoughts you invite can enter. Start to feel that place once you have relaxed through the breathing. It may be a fireside you know well, or a place in nature, like a beach, meadow, river, wood or hillside. Perhaps it's a room you had as a child or a place you went and felt good. Wherever it is, go there now. As you walk towards it, notice how much more solid it becomes as you enter it from the here and now.

Be aware of the colours around you and the textures of the things you touch. If you are on the beach, pick up some sand and feel it trickling through your fingers. If you are in a wood, feel the bark of the tree and watch the insects scurrying in the cracks. Maybe you can feel a cool breeze from the sea or perhaps you can feel the warming sun on your back.

Once you are there, safe, calm and relaxed you can allow anyone else you want to join you. Remember that you are in control of this situation and that you can stop whenever you want. Whenever you want to stop, just become aware of your body and your real surroundings. Focus on your breathing again and slowly open your eyes. You may feel a little woozy at first if you are not used to doing visualisations but once everything comes into focus, you will feel fine. Just take things easy for a moment or two and drink some water.

The Inner Child

Get comfortable, as described above, close your eyes, breathe and go to your safe, happy place in your head. Once you are completely calm and relaxed look around and notice yourself as a young child playing a few steps away. Call yourself by name – it might be a special name you had for yourself as a child or the name you go by now. Hold out your hands, so that the child knows you are friendly and make sure that you are smiling at him or her. Beckon him or her over to you.

How old is the child? Is s/he smiling, playing, laughing or crying? If so, what is making him or her feel that way? Ask him or her to tell you how they feel in the simple, three word way we described. If the child is too emotional to speak, just feel how s/he is feeling and tell him or her that it's OK to feel that way.

Ask the child if there is anything you, as an adult, can do for him or her. You will know what s/he wants instinctively. Are you able to give him or her what she needs? You almost certainly are, or you wouldn 't have allowed yourself to meet him or her in this way. It might be a hug. It might be to tell him or her that everything turned out OK – 'look at me now'. It might be to play.

Once you have done whatever it is you need to do, tell him or her that you are going to come back often and that they will never be lonely or without a playmate again, then slowly leave the place, making sure that the child knows you are coming back. You could even take the child with you if they want to come. Just pick them up and go back up the path to where you were first.

Once you have got used to talking to your inner child you will love being with them and will want to spend more time with them. Try meeting up at least twice a week. As you meet, you will probably find that the child changes and becomes generally happier. You can give the child what it needs both in your visualisations and in life. If you didn't play much as a child, you might want to play now. Treat your inner child to a go on the swings, the carousel or play roly poly down a bank. Don't worry about how you look or what others might think; remember that what anyone else thinks doesn 't matter. You may find that your inner child likes getting into his or her pyjamas after work and reading, while cuddling a favourite animal. Whatever it is, go for it!

Self-Esteem

These visualisations are to boost your confidence in yourself and raise your self-esteem. As with the Inner Child, prepare yourself as described at the beginning and go to your special place, where you will feel calm and relaxed.

To have self-esteem, you need to know yourself and what you need and want out of life to make you happy. You have filled out your SWOON chart and know what your values are and, most importantly, what your purpose is in life. To achieve your purpose, you have probably set yourself some goals, so now you are going to picture yourself achieving those goals.

Let's say that a goal is to lose some weight. Once you are in your special place, you find a full length mirror and you go up to it but instead of seeing yourself as you are, you see yourself as you would like to be. You are wearing a really flattering outfit and you look healthy and happy, with shining hair and glowing skin. Suddenly you realise that your very best friends are there and they are so proud of you and how well you look. As you mingle with them, you become aware that you are walking taller and that you are radiating desirability. People are gravitating towards you and can't seem to take their eyes off you. When you have had enough of the adulation, walk back to where you started and gradually come back to the real world.

Do this every day for 21 days, preferably before meal times and will find yourself unconsciously choosing healthier food and not wanting things you know pile on the weight. You will find yourself drinking more water and wanting to increase your exercise levels. Day by day, you will start to become slimmer and healthier as you approach your goal.

Or, maybe you would like to become more assertive. Go to your special place and gradually notice that there is someone else there, someone who you perhaps always defer to, someone you find it difficult to refuse, even if you already have enough on your plate. It might be a work colleague or your boss or a parent, partner or friend. Whoever it is, they are there to ask you to do something for them and you really don't want to do it.

Now they are in your special place they can't bully, frighten or cajole you into doing anything you don't want to do. They are on your turf and have to abide by your rules.

Now, visualise them asking you to do whatever it is you know they are going to ask you or what they have asked you to do before. It could be anything from cleaning to writing reports for them. Look them in the eye in an open and pleasant way and say 'No'. Don't say 'I'm sorry.' Just say 'No' firmly and clearly and make your body language mirror your word, shake your head and put your hand in a warding off position. Visualise their response as being accepting. You can elaborate on 'No' if you need to, such as, 'I have plans for tonight' or 'I am taking my children swimming on Saturday.' Just don't make excuses and don't vary from the 'No' theme. Do this every day for 21 days. Once you can stand up for yourself you will respect yourself more.

Silencing the Inner Critic

We discussed the inner critic and by now you may have realised who your harshest critic is. It may be a parent, a partner, friend or a teacher. Whoever it is, you have to stop them preventing you from living the life you want to live.

Go to your special place and get comfortable. As you did in the last visualisation, invite your Inner Critic into your space and ask them to sit down. Now remember a time when you didn't do something because their voice stopped you. As you say that you are going to do this particular thing, which you very much want to do, imagine what they say; they just go on and on about how bad it is and how people will think you are stupid or too old or whatever. It's such a constant whining! But, hold on, there are some balloons nearby and you get them to pick one up and inhale some of the air inside. It's a helium balloon and their voice gets higher and higher until you can't hear it at all. They look so funny opening and shutting their mouth with no noise coming out that you start to laugh and then you laugh and laugh because you just can't hear them! Do this with every critical voice you hear and replace the criticism with your own laughter.

Your Ideal Life

We mentioned in the text that some schools of thought believe that it is possible to create your own reality. We explore this more in other books but, if you feel ready to really change your life, you can start by visualising your perfect future. There are literally thousands of visualisations to choose from but we are going to start with letting go of things in the past that are holding you back.

Go to your special place, as before, and become calm and relaxed. Now think of attitudes you have had which have anchored you to a life path you don't really want. You will find a pad and a pencil nearby – not a pen, a pencil. On the pad write down all the things which have held you back. These may be fear, insecurity, depression, obedience or addiction. Or you may have phrases to write down, such as 'I can't say No' 'or I'm too old/fat/stupid'. Once you have written them down, rip the sheet out of the pad, then screw it into a ball. There's a bonfire nearby. Throw the balls of paper into the fire and watch them disappear.

Now, on a beautiful canvas you find nearby you write in beautiful handwriting, with huge letters, whatever it is you can do without those limiting words or phrases from the past. Hang the canvas on the wall/a nearby tree or off a rock, wherever your special place is, so that you see it every time you visit.

Write 'I am successful/courageous/optimistic/healthy/enthusi-astic' – whatever it is that you want to be. As we say in the text, don't expect to go from zero to hero in one session. The point is that you have to *believe* that you are these things. Start with baby steps and you will find that your baby steps have soon become several giant steps. Do this every day for the rest of your life and you will become that person.

For specific goals, visualise them in minute detail. For example, you may want to get a new job and you are finding it difficult. When you are in your special place, with your canvas hanging nearby, see yourself in the new job. Visualise your desk, your computer, your tool kit, the pictures you have stuck to the wall – including a mini version of your canvas – your coat behind the door – anything that symbolizes your new place of work. Now read all the cards from friends congratulating you on your new job; they are all so proud of you and knew that you would do it. New work colleagues or clients keep popping up to say how pleased they are that you have made the move.

Do this every day while you are looking for work and you'll soon find the right job for you, even if it is unpaid. Remember what we said about identifying your needs. We always get what we ask for eventually; it may just be in a different form from the one we expected.

Exercises

For those of you who find visualisation harder, it might be an idea to start with some exercises. All you need for these are pen, paper and some self-knowledge. Using your EI Journal is a good idea, as you can look back in time and see how far how you've moved on and what blocks you have shifted.

Self-Esteem

This exercise helps you to see what your mental blockages are and how you can get round them – or better still, eradicate them.

Write down the following questions, leaving enough space to answer them in your own words. They are all about your life and what would make you happy, so just be honest. Also, read the beginning of the statement and then write the end of it quickly and without thinking. Sometimes, what you write will surprise you.

If I had the confidence, I would change my life by

If I knew I couldn't fail, I would

If I felt confident enough, I would stop doing/accepting

If I knew that everyone would support me in my decision, I would

The answers to these questions should give you your 'reasons' for not living your life how you would really like to live it. In your EI journal, write down each 'reason' and then examine it, as shown in SWOON.

Communicating With Others and Building Rapport

It is almost certain that your relationships are the most important things in your life, whoever they are with. In a life filled with values, the measure of success should be on relationships and not material wealth or business success. Effective communication with oneself and others is what Emotional Intelligence is all about. The following exercises will help you to communicate better:

- When asked a question or when tempted to have your say in any interaction, count to 10 first
- Only say positive things but stay truthful. If asked 'Does my bum look big in this?' and it does, either suggest another outfit or, if the bum in question is going to look big in anything, draw attention to how much the colour suits her.
- Smile as much as you can without looking freaky. Your body language is more important than what you say, remember.
- Wear 'approachable' colours. Black looks professional but it can also be off-putting. Try blues and greens for a change.
- Initiate conversation. There's always the weather! The other person may be keen to talk but be even more scared than you are.

Do the above for a week and write down your results in your EI journal. You will be amazed at how much better people are responding to you. Like attracts like and if you give off 'prickly' that is what you'll attract. Conversely, give off open and friendly and that is what you'll attract.

If you're having trouble with a relationship and you want to repair it, try the following:

- Be direct and ask for what you want out of the relationship. The other person my be oblivious to the fact that you would like to see more (or less) of them and would like the same only you were both too scared to say so. People appreciate honesty much more than we give them credit for.

- Close both eyes. There was a family saying that to make a friend you should close one eye to their faults and to keep a friend, you should close both. It's very apt. What we're saying is that no-one is perfect and, even if they are, they aren't going to perfectly meet our expectations. For example, you might think that you're careful with money, maybe because it was in short supply when you were younger. To you it is a virtue, while to someone else you might just be a tightwad. It doesn't mean to say that they don't want to spend time with you, just that it is one of your characteristics and they have to accept it if they want to keep you as a friend. Always try and make allowances for other people's motivations. There are always two sides in any relationship. It just comes back to your perceptions.

- Don't allow grievances to fester, as they can grow over time. Once you have both calmed down, look at what caused the disagreement and then apologise for your part in it. If you really and truly are in no way to blame (which is unlikely, even if the blame could have been a perception by the other person) then state your case clearly and non-judgmentally in writing. It is up to you whether you send the letter. Sometimes even the act of writing everything down helps you to get a clear perspective. If you feel that the differences are too big to overcome then cut your ties, if you can, and put the relationship behind you. It is impossible to put a relationship in the past if you harp on about it, discuss it with other friends or colleagues or don 't forgive the other person, so don't be surprised in those circumstances to find it holding you back. But, remember that everything happens in small steps. You are not going to forget a lover, old friend or family member overnight, so don't be hard on yourself when you can't.

- Treat people with respect. If you do what you say you are going to do, don't betray confidences and don't let people down at the last minute, then they will respect you and want to be your friend. Also, remember that family members should be accorded the same respect. Just because he's your brother, it doesn't give you the right to treat him badly.

Self-Assessment Interpretations

Are you emotionally intelligent?

Scores

1/. a] 3,   b] 2,   c] 1   _____

2/. a] 3,   b] 2,   c] 1   _____

3/. a] 2,   b] 1,   c] 3   _____

4/. a] 1,   b] 3,   c] 2   _____

5/. a] 2,   b] 1,   c] 3   _____

6/. a] 3,   b] 1,   c] 2   _____

7/. a] 3,   b] 1,   c] 2   _____

8/. a] 2,   b] 3,   c] 1   _____

9/. a] 3,   b] 2,   c] 1   _____

10/. a] 3,   b] 1,   c] 2   _____

11/. a] 1,   b] 3,   c] 2   _____

12/. a] 1,   b] 2,   c] 3   _____

Total   _____

12 - 19

You are ill-at-ease with your emotions and for all your apparent good intentions you take refuge in 'appropriate' responses and often bland submissiveness. If you cannot confront your emotions honestly, acknowledging that they are valid, however 'good' or 'bad' they are, you can only repress them or simulate a proper response rather than turning them to constructive use. Remember that all emotions have been felt before and are, to a greater or lesser extent, common to all human beings. Repressing emotions can result in mental and physical illness and fiercely held convictions, which are not emotionally true, are often moralistic dogmatism.

20 - 27 Your robust attempts to master your emotions are praiseworthy but frequently ill-judged and unsympathetic. You defend yourself from 'unworthy' emotions by simulating appropriate responses, but you tend to give rent-free space in your head and mind to people and things which were considered, understood and consigned to the emotional data-bank for subsequent use. Try *allowing* emotions in, even emotions which seem unworthy – anger, fear, frailty, depression, anxiety – to harmless contexts such as when listening to music or watching films.

28 - 36

You have no problems in accepting and using your emotions when appropriate, while imposing restraint on destructive impulses. You are comfortable with your natural responses where they serve their turn and know how to channel their useful physiological consequences to best effects.

How well do you know – and like - yourself?

Scores

1/. a] 2,   b] 3,   c] 1   _____

2/. a] 3,   b] 1,   c] 2   _____

3/. a] 3,   b] 2,   c] 1   _____

4/. a] 3,   b] 2,   c] 1   _____

5/. a] 3,   b] 1,   c] 2   _____

6/. a] 1,   b] 3,   c] 2   _____

7/. a] 3,   b] 2,   c] 1   _____

8/. a] 2,   b] 3,   c] 1   _____

9/. a] 3,   b] 2,   c] 1   _____

10/. a] 2,   b] 1,   c] 3   _____

11/. a] 1,   b] 2,   c] 3   _____

12/. a] 3,   b] 1,   c] 2   _____

Total   _____

12 - 18

Come on... You aren't really that bad. Look at yourself in a mirror. Marvel at the way in which every minute complex part of you functions, then tell me that you are not remarkable and wonderful. All this dislike of others is really founded upon nothing more than dislike of yourself. Beautiful, rich and successful people can still feel pain, you know, and insecurity. Your smile or enthusiastic help could make you valuable even to them. Disapproval and dislike should be reasoned and specific. Where it is general, it speaks of mistrust of your own nature not of others.

19 - 27

Steady now... You certainly accept what you think you are but are not sure whether that image tallies with the real you – fallible, frail, uncertain, mortal man or woman? Your aggression and assertiveness seem to speak rather more of poor self-image and of confidence in a projection. Whereas those in category 12 - 18 will have the humility to do something about it however, you may find rather more difficulty in developing an accurate appreciation of yourself. The projection after all, is popular enough and you never need to consider all those inconvenient little flaws that make you human. This in turn makes you tolerant of the same flaws in others.

28 - 36

You do not have to assert yourself – which is to say, defend yourself – in order to inspire confidence. Your positive self-image, founded upon reality, not a projection, will readily communicate itself to others. You appear to be happy in your own skin. It is contagious.

How Much Self-Confidence Do You Have?

Scores

1/. a] 2,   b] 3,   c] 1 _____

2/. a] 3,   b] 2,   c] 1 _____

3/. a] 3,   b] 2,   c] 1 _____

4/. a] 3,   b] 1,   c] 2 _____

5/. a] 2,   b] 3,   c] 1 _____

6/. a] 2,   b] 1,   c] 3 _____

7/. a] 1,   b] 2,   c] 3 _____

8/. a] 3,   b] 2,   c] 1 _____

9/. a] 3,   b] 2,   c] 1 _____

10/. a] 2,   b] 3,   c] 1 _____

11/. a] 1,   b] 2,   c] 3 _____

12/. a] 1,   b] 3,   c] 2 _____

Total _____

12 - 19

You seem to have attained a balance between self-love and self-awareness, assurance and introspection. You are confidant yet not so overweening so as to have banished sensitivity towards others. You are resilient yet considerate and well equipped to survive emotional turmoil because you are in touch with your own inner self.

20 - 27

Your timidity is a handicap, your mistrust of yourself a conditioned reflex inhibiting you from emotionally intelligent communicative responses. You need to remind yourself that there are many people who could benefit from your good ways. You need to count your many achievements and blessings. You need to look at the many people less fortunate, weaker, less intelligent and less attractive than yourself and train and develop your own emotional intelligence to lead you to take responsibility and to make a positive contribution to your community, your environment and your own welfare. If your want of self-worth is a consequence of an unappreciative partner or family, look to the outside world in order to exercise your emotional intelligence.

28 - 36

Quite the life and soul of the party, confident, opinionated, can be tetchy and ebullient, you may fool yourself, but we have our suspicions. Do you really notice other people? Do you think their emotions even related to yours? You have programed yourself to react confidently and assuredly to most circumstance but it is time that you considered your own frailties, however well disguised, and relate them to those of others.

Do You Know what Your Values Are?

Scores

1/. a] 1,   b] 3,   c] 2   _____

2/. a] 2,   b] 3,   c] 1   _____

3/. a] 3,   b] 1,   c] 2   _____

4/. a] 2,   b] 1,   c] 3   _____

5/. a] 2,   b] 3,   c] 1   _____

6/. a] 2,   b] 1,   c] 3   _____

7/. a] 3,   b] 2,   c] 1   _____

8/. a] 2,   b] 3,   c] 1   _____

9/. a] 3,   b] 2,   c] 1   _____

10/. a] 3,   b] 1,   c] 2   _____

11/. a] 1,   b] 2,   c] 3   _____

12/. a] 3,   b] 2,   c] 1   _____

Total   _____

12 - 19

It is sad to be so independent yet so aggressive and moody as to alienate most people upon whom you might depend someday or sometime. Resentment, futile worry, dwelling upon grievances and in need of constant external stimulus, your every need makes you a victim and so the cycle goes on. Only you can break it. Your temperament of course, is in part innate, but the emotionally intelligent 'born winner' starts by recognizing this. Worrying has a purpose but it also has its place. Love is wonderful, but when it is not around, there is more to life. Stubbornness, although splendid when applied to difficult tasks, has no merit whatsoever when applied to ordinary social interactions. Use your own compartmentalizing techniques to best effect. Devote set times to resolving the causes of your worry, other times to reading and becoming what other people see you as. Above all, devote time to your journal, silence, to walking or meditating. Make life for yourself and so recognize that others have their own lives and cannot devote them to you.

20 - 27

Communicative, gregarious when necessary, yet unafraid of silence and solitude, you seem to be sufficiently confident at once to assert yourself without insecure aggression where suitable and to be happy in your own skin even when alone.

28 - 36

You seem fairly independent, assertive and constantly busy, but it would seem that, in your own way, you are tied up in yourself and dependent upon others' responses to you as favorable or unfavorable – as the eternal victim. It is time to take a holiday from the non-stop assertion of self. After all, if you are content with your self, why do you have a need for assertion? Independence, true independence, may be concerned with others' welfare, but not with the opinions of others.

Is Your Relationship in Danger of Flooding?

Scores

1/. a] 1,   b] 2,   c] 3   _____

2/. a] 1,   b] 2,   c] 3   _____

3/. a] 3,   b] 1,   c] 2   _____

4/. a] 1,   b] 3,   c] 2   _____

5/. a] 3,   b] 2,   c] 1   _____

6/. a] 1,   b] 3,   c] 2   _____

7/. a] 1,   b] 2,   c] 3   _____

8/. a] 2,   b] 1,   c] 3   _____

9/. a] 2,   b] 1,   c] 3   _____

10/. a] 3,   b] 1,   c] 2   _____

11/. a] 1,   b] 2,   c] 3   _____

12/. a] 1,   b] 3,   c] 2   _____

Total   _____

12 - 19 There are two words, which the emotionally intelligent should delete from their vocabulary, because they are dangerous, destructive lies. The words are "always" and "never". No one is "always" or "never" anything. People have irritating habits, destructive vices, bad traits which surface from time to time, insecurities which manifest themselves as assertiveness, fears which emerge disguised as certainties, prejudices founded on ignorance, but they are people, not monsters for all of this.

Your responses – even to overtures of peace and acts of kindness – are pre-programmed to fight-or-flight. It may be too late for you to banish these lies but, if your relationship is worth saving – and most are – in one form or another then list your partner's qualities and praise them, remind yourself of all the reasons that you got together in the first place, count your blessings and gently communicate your distress whenever it arises. Be ready to say "sorry" and to make concessions over trivial matters. Use lots of 'I feel' sentences and do lots of non-threatening touching.

Develop a code for your own purposes or, if possible, to be shared with your partner, in order to identify upsurges of anger or irritation or even anxiety and panic. Break the cycle whenever possible by recognizing that you are both badly bruised and in need of very gentle handling.

20 - 27

The illusions of "always" and "never" detailed above often result in disappointment and disillusion. The notion that your lover is perfect, wonderful, marvellous and superhuman is natural in the first emotional flush or deluge which we call falling in love, but it is nonetheless untrue, for that, and each subsequent, inevitable disillusion, is seen, unjustly, as a betrayal. Romance is just that, romancing or telling stories and, on its own is a poor basis for a relationship. Love is lovely – make the most of it – but also recognize that the more you idealize the more bitter and cruel it

will become. It is easy to love a fictional character. It's a lot harder
to muddle along with a fellow human being.

28 - 36
There is no danger of flooding here – merely perhaps of compla-
cency – but at least you can choose to inject gallantry, comedy,
games and romance into your relationship when you want to
without feeling that, by doing so, you are making concessions.

Acknowledgements

We would like to acknowledge the works and quotes of the following people:

Aristotle, Ivy Baker-Priest, Reuven Bar-On, Keith Beasley, Chris Bell, Michael Boase, Lucia Cappachine, David Caruso, Francesca Cassini, Charles Darwin, John Donne, Albert Einstein, Robert Emmerling, Ralph Waldo Emerson, Erik Erikson, Antoine de St Exupéry, Viktor Frankl, Sigmund Freud, Mahatma Ghandi, Johann Wolfgang von Goethe, Samuel Goldwyn, Steve Hein, Steve Jobs, Carl Gustav Jung, Carl Lans, Madonna, Barry Mason, John Mayer, Daphne Du Maurier, A A Milne, Margaret Mitchell, Reinhold Niebuhr, Satchel Paige, Plato, Les Reed, Gene Roddenberry, Leon Russell, Peter Salovey, Friedrich Schiller, Mark Slaski, Byron Stock, Mark Twain, Mae West, Oscar Wilde, Tom Wolfe.

Bibliography and Recommended Reading

Arnold Bennett *How To Live On 24 Hours A Day* (published by Shambling Gate Press)

Robin Casarjian *Houses of Healing* (published by Lionheart Foundation)

Dr Daniel Goleman *Emotional Intelligence* (published by Bantam) (the 10th Anniversary Edition is more up to date)

Esther & Jerry Hicks *Ask And It Is Given* (published by Hay House)

Carl Gustav Jung *The Archetypes And The Collective Unconscious* and *The Undiscovered Self* (both published by Princeton University Press)

Elizabeth Kübler-Ross *Working It Through* (published by Scribner)

George Orwell *Animal Farm* (published by Plume)

[1] It costs £38,000 annually to keep a man in prison.

BOOKS

O is a symbol of the world, of oneness and unity. In different cultures it also means the "eye," symbolizing knowledge and insight. We aim to publish books that are accessible, constructive and that challenge accepted opinion, both that of academia and the "moral majority."

Our books are available in all good English language bookstores worldwide. If you don't see the book on the shelves ask the bookstore to order it for you, quoting the ISBN number and title. Alternatively you can order online (all major online retail sites carry our titles) or contact the distributor in the relevant country, listed on the copyright page.

See our website **www.o-books.net** for a full list of over 500 titles, growing by 100 a year.

And tune in to myspiritradio.com for our book review radio show, hosted by June-Elleni Laine, where you can listen to the authors discussing their books.

mySpiritRadio

Printed and bound by CPI Group (UK) Ltd, Croydon, CR0 4YY